MAKE ME A COCKTAIL

AT CHRISTMAS

AUTHOR
Nick Wilkins

EDITOR
Astrid Bowser

Copyright © 2019 Nick Wilkins

All rights reserved.

ISBN: 9781709438844

Introduction

Makemeacocktail.com is the world's biggest and best cocktail resource! Over the years, the Make Me A Cocktail community has created and shared over 3,500 inspiring, classic and occasionally daring cocktail concoctions for fellow enthusiasts to recreate at simply at home, for entertaining guests at parties or making memorable, unique events.

We here at Make Me A Cocktail have collated, tried, tested and been inspired by a host of amazing cocktails. From the classics to the new age crazy concoctions, we've enjoyed seeing what new directions bartenders and cocktail enthusiasts are taking.

For our first Make Me A Cocktail book, we've collated our top cocktails for the festive period. We've raided our cupboards, scoured the internet and drank far too many Mince Pie Martinis, to discover, create and be amazed by the creativity we have found, to combine the wonderful Christmas Cocktails contained in this book.

We hope you enjoy trying some of the selected cocktails as much as we did choosing and tasting them. We have hopefully included something to intrigue and inspire everyone over this wonderful time of the year to compliment your favourite choice of tipple, mood or occasion!

Nick
Make Me A Cocktailer

Contents

The Blurbs

Introduction	i
Guide to Cocktail Preparation	5
Equipment	6
Techniques	7
Conversions	8
Drink Responsibly	8
Online Community	9
Ingredients Index	80

The Cocktails

Santa's Stiff Hot Chocolate	10
Mince Pie Martini	12
Bitter Orange Cardamom Martini	14
Sassy Little Elf	16
Jean Gabin	18
Moscow Reindeer	20
Tequila Winter Sunrise	22
Rudolph's Red Nose	24
White Russian Christmas	26
Warm Bourbon Cider	28
Chocolate Orange Cocktail	30
Mulled Pear and Cranberry Punch	32
Winter Sidecar	34
Champagne Comme-il-faut	36
Santa's Nightcap	38
Winter Pimms Punch	40
Christmas Cosmopolitan	42
Pimped Up Prosecco	44
Christmas Snowball	46
Glogg	48
Baby Bellini	50
Winter Whiskey Sour	52
The North Pole	54
Hot Peppermint Patty	56
Snowball	58
Brandy Eggnog	60
Christmas Pudding Sour	62
Christmas Punch	64
Christmas Coffee	66
Hot Buttered Rum	68
Pumpkin Latte	70
Martin's Rum	72
Mocha Eggnog Latte	74
Mimosa	76
Christmas Baubles	78

Guide To Cocktail Preparation

The cocktail world is often shrouded with ubiquitous bartenders setting light to the oils from lemon rinds over carefully crafted perfectly balanced iced glasses, sprinkling 'just a dash' of bitters to enhance the aromas from the first sip of their new age concoction.

But we're here to tell you it doesn't need to be that way. Throw the right proportions of the ingredients into a cocktail shaker with ice, shake a little then strain. You'll produce delicious cocktails time and time again. Garnish with an orange slice and your friends will think you're the next Tom Cruise from that wonderful 80's film Cocktail. Grate some nutmeg garnish and you're the next world class bartender.

However, all drinks do need some basics to get you going, and here we list some simple equipment you'll need, and some simple terminology and techniques to blaze your own path to cocktail stardom. Cocktails are to be enjoyed, so have fun and play with the flavours you've got hand. You never know, you may create a new classic for the world to enjoy!

Equipment

Cocktail Shaker

You can't get far with most cocktails without the staple of any personal home bar - the cocktail shaker. Add some ice to the ingredients within, shake for 10-15 seconds and strain into the required glass. Simple.

Strainer

Right after the cocktail shaker comes the strainer. Some shakers have a basic strainer built in, but to catch all those ice lumps or fruit pieces you don't want in your finished product, a simple strainer suffices.

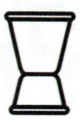

Jigger

To get the right balance of flavours you need the right proportions of the ingredients, and most of the time that'll be in the form of measuring the liquid in a jigger. They usually come in 25ml and 50ml variations, and we've tried to keep our cocktails in this book within that range.

Techniques

SHAKING

"Just make sure the top stays on" as my old bartending mentor used to say. And I part that knowledge onto you now. But along with that, you'll want to break up the ice into smaller particles, chilling the contents and combining up the flavours. Shaking for around 10-15 seconds is usually sufficient, you'll feel the outside of the shaker become really cold and frosted.

STIRRING

I'm not sure we need to give you an introduction to what this means, but if you want to get all cocktail geeky, then stirring allows you to chill drinks, or combine flavours, without bubbling up or bruising the ingredients. It also allows you to mix fizzy elements such as champagne or soda. Twizzle away for 10-15 seconds and you should be good to go.

MUDDLING

Muddling is such a great descriptive word, literally muddling or mashing the flavours up. You don't need a muddler, a good hard muddle with the end of a small rolling pin might suffice, but a muddler helps really release those flavours. Simply grind and twist whatever you're muddling a few times to get the juices and oils released from the ingredients.

Conversions

In this book we've used a consistent millimeter measurement throughout, or explanatory measurements where appropriate. You can easily swap in for oz using the conversion below:

ML	OZ
25	0.9
50	1.8
60	2.1
70	2.5
100	3.5
500	17.5

Drink Responsibly

Always drink alcohol responsibly and in moderation, knowing your limits and never on an empty stomach. In this book we've collated some amazing cocktails, some which are alcohol free, and others that are on the stronger side of the ABV line. Please be sensible when consuming large amount of alcohol and if in any doubt refer to resources such as;

https://responsibledrinking.eu
https://www.drinkaware.co.uk
http://www.responsibledrinking.org
https://www.drinkinmoderation.org

ONLINE COMMUNITY

This book was created thanks to inspiration from the wonderful community makemeacocktail.com - The World's Best Cocktail Resource. We'd love for you to share your creations from this book on social media or with us at Make Me A Cocktail. We love to see what you all create from the classics to the complex and the crazy!

Makemeacocktail.com contains thousands of recipes for you to try, but also has our unique My Bar feature, allowing you to enter what you have in your cupboards at home so we can show you what you can make from what you have. Hey, we'll even recommend what to buy next to increase your cocktail making potential.

Register online for free to join the community and you can start to create lists of your favourite cocktails, subscribe to our bi-weekly ingredient deep dive and be part of our vibrant and welcoming online community. We created the site for people just like you, to help you create, inspire, and entertain friends and family alike with the wonderful concoctions you can learn to make.

- 🌐 makemeacocktail.com
- 🐦 @makeacocktail
- 📘 /makemeacocktail
- 📌 /makemeacocktail
- 📷 /makemeacocktail

Santa's Stiff Hot Chocolate

Santa's favourite drink to come home to after a hard day's work out in the cold winter's night delivering presents. Mrs. Claus kept the recipe secret.... until now!

Ingredients
Serves 2

- 50 ML **DARK RUM**
- 1 TBSP **HONEY**
- 500 ML **MILK**
- ¼ TSP **VANILLA ESSENCE**
- 3 TSP **BROWN SUGAR**
- ½ STICK **CINNAMON**
- ½ CUP **CHOCOLATE**

SWEET

LONG

WARMING

Method

In a saucepan over a low heat, add the milk, honey, sugar and ½ cinnamon stick. Grate the chocolate into this mix and cook until the chocolate is melted. Don't rush and heat up the milk too quickly, or you risk burning the milk and not infusing the flavours enough.

Once melted, take off the heat to add the vanilla essence and the rum. Whisk the mixture before straining into the glass. Garnish on top with some whipped cream, mini marshmallows and chocolate shavings to serve while hot.

If available, add a vanilla pod into the milk mixture when cooking. It gives a stronger infused vanilla kick to the finished drink.

Mince Pie Martini

We have done it. Make Me A Cocktail have found a martini that truly smells and tastes like Christmas, with a kick! Get ready to impress your guests this festive season!

Ingredients
Serves 1

- 25 ML **GIN**
- 50 ML **DARK RUM**
- 25 ML **SWEET RED VERMOUTH**
- 50 G **MINCEMEAT**
- 100 G **SUGAR**
- 100 ML **WATER**

STRONG

SOHPISTICATED

IMPRESS

Method

First make a mincemeat syrup for use in the cocktail. Boil 100g sugar with 50g mincemeat and 100ml of water. Bring to the boil before cooling and straining. This will make a fairly large batch that can be stored in the fridge for later use.

Take a cocktail glass and dampen the edges with the mincemeat syrup, before dipping in some mixed spice to rim the glass. In a cocktail shaker mix 25 ml of the mincemeat syrup with the gin, vermouth and dark rum with ice and shake for 20 seconds. Strain into the cocktail glass and serve.

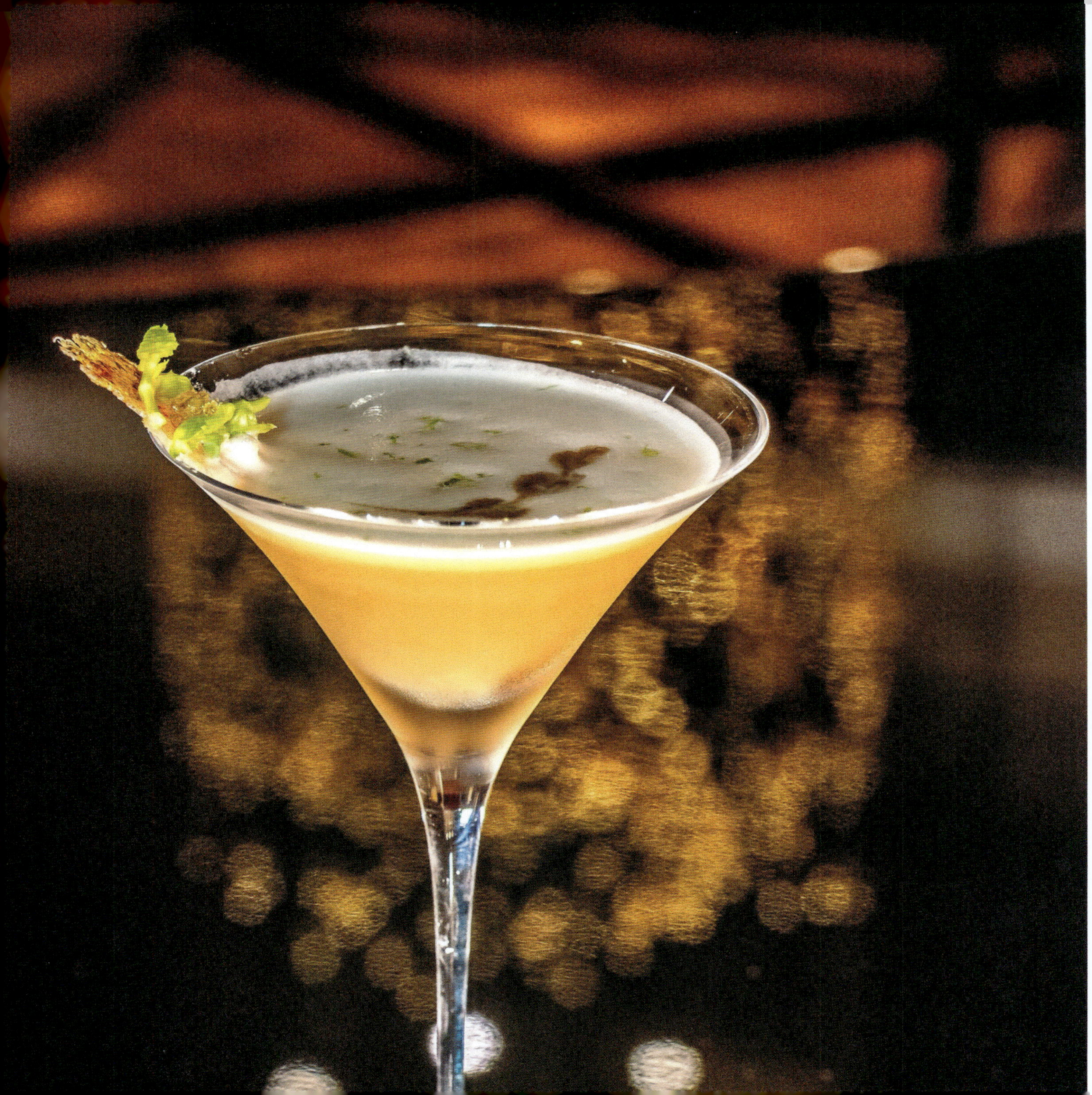

Bitter Orange And Cardamom Martini

Infused with that wonderful aroma of orange and spices reminiscent of Christmas, this delightful martini will be sure to get any festive party started!

Ingredients
Serves 1

- 60 ML **VODKA**
- 20 ML **COINTREAU**
- 70 ML **LEMON JUICE**
- 1 TBSP **MARMALADE**
- 2 **CARDAMOM PODS**

DECADANT

SPICE

CITRUS

Method

In a small saucepan add the marmalade and heat up gently - you don't want it to boil, simply warm up to make the marmalade runny. Add in the cardamom pods and crush to release their flavour. Let it combine for a couple of minutes before taking the saucepan off the heat and leave to cool. Once cooled add the Cointreau, lemon juice and vodka to a mixing glass and add in the marmalade cardamom mixture. Stir to combine, ensuring you mix the liquids through the marmalade.

To serve take a chilled martini glass and add a dollop of marmalade to the bottom, before pouring in the mixture. Serve with a cardamom pod floating on top and an orange segment on a twizzle stick.

To maximise enjoyment time and to ensure you don't run dry, pre-make a batch of the cardamom infused marmalade before-hand. Once combined it will last for a couple of days in the fridge.

Sassy Little Elf

For those who really want to impress their guests at Christmas with something a little different! This unusual vodka based liqueur is blended with exotic fruits and is a striking pink colour!

Ingredients
Serves 1

- 60 ML **X RATED FUSION LIQUEUR**
- 45 ML **GUAVA JUICE**
- 15 ML **LEMON JUICE**
- 30 ML **HALF AND HALF**

IMPRESS

SOPHISTICATED

PARTY

Method

Shake the X Rated Fusion Liqueur, guava juice, lemon juice and Half and Half in a cocktail shaker with ice. Shake well for 10-15 seconds or until the outside of the shaker becomes frosted. Strain into cocktail glass. Garnish with a lemon rind twist and a mini candy cane.

Half and Half is half cream, half milk. Simple to make up if you don't have the exact ingredient!

Jean Gabin

Looking for a naughty festive night cap that wins over the traditional hot chocolate? This classic created in 1986 by Charles Schumann is the perfect choice.

Ingredients
Serves 1

- 25 ML **DARK RUM**
- 20 ML **CALVADOS**
- 25 ML **MILK**
- 1 TBSP **MAPLE SYRUP**
- GRATING **NUTMEG**

CLASSIC

WARMING

IMPRESS

Method

First heat up the milk in a pan. While that is going on heat the maple syrup, calvados and dark rum in another (sorry for the washing up). Pour in the hot milk to the syrup, calvados and rum before mixing and serving in an Irish coffee glass.

To finish, sprinkle some nutmeg over the top.

Save yourself the effort of heating multiple times for more than one serving, and make a few of these in one go.

Moscow Reindeer Cocktail

The heat of the fiery ginger beer and vodka and the coolness of crushed ice and mint makes this simple cocktail a winter winner at any time of the day!

Ingredients
Serves 1

- 50 ML **VODKA**
- 20 ML **LIME JUICE**
- 200 ML **FIERY GINGER BEER**
- 10 **MINT LEAVES**

SIMPLE

FAST

LONG

Method

Muddle the mint leaves in a bottom of the serving glass with a little crushed ice. Top up with the crushed ice before pouring in the vodka and lime juice. Top up with ginger beer, garnish with a couple of mint leaves and biodegradable straw before serving.

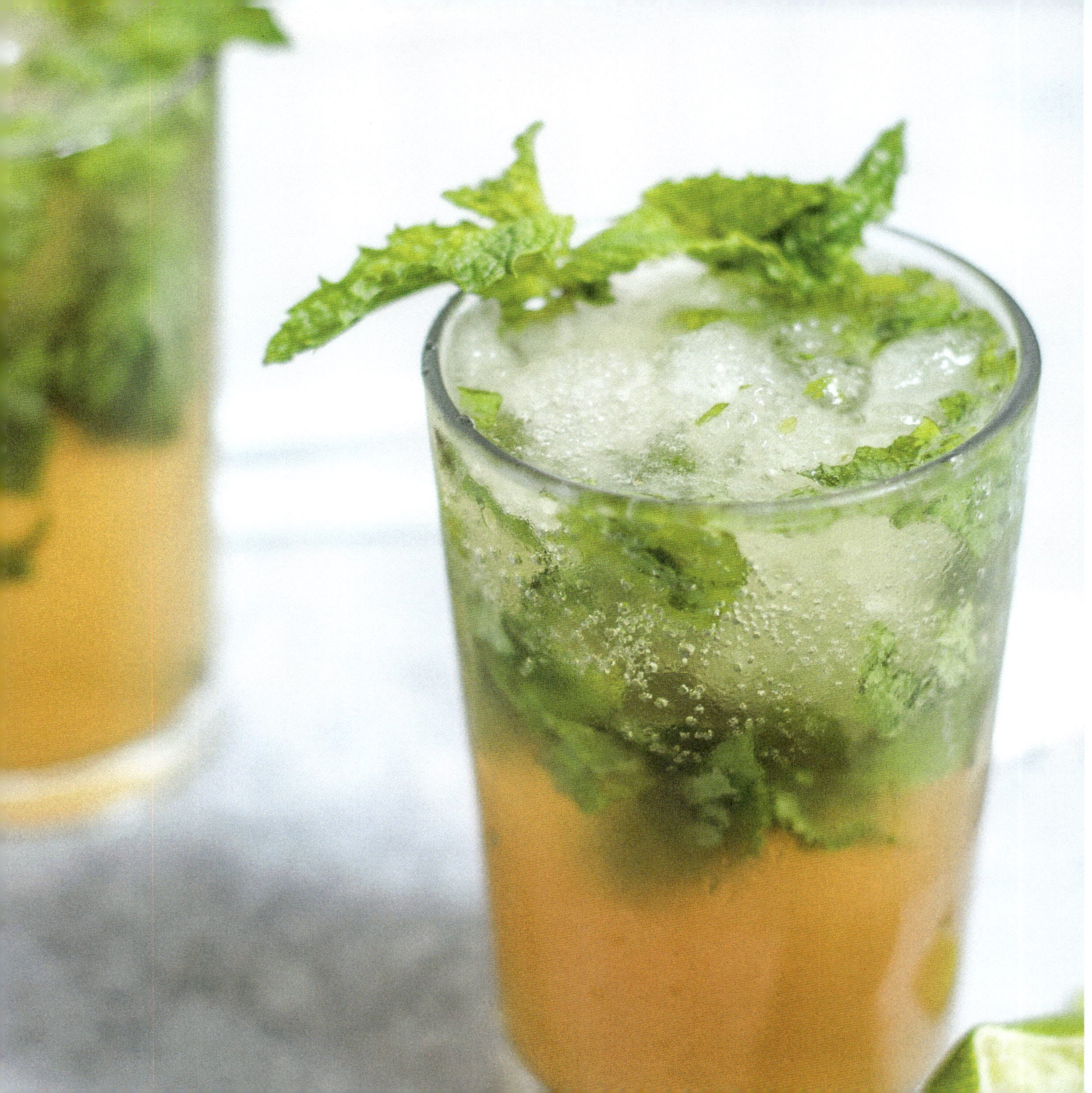

Tequila Winter Sunrise

When the cold nights and winter draws in, we sometimes yearn for that summer sun to come back round quickly! A chilly and slightly more adventurous take on the classic Tequila Sunrise should help you bring the sunshine to any occasion in winter! Unless of course you are a Make Me A Cocktail enthusiast from Australia, this one's for you!

Ingredients
Serves 1

- 25 ML **TEQUILA**
- 25 ML **ORANGE LIQUEUR**
- 50 ML **ORANGE JUICE**
- 50 ML **CRANBERRY JUICE**
- SQUEEZE **LIME**
- 2 TBSP **POMEGRANATE SYRUP**

PARTY

LONG

EXTRAVAGENT

Method

Pour the tequila, then the orange liqueur, orange juice and cranberry juice into a hurricane glass with ice (in that order). Gently pour the pomegranate syrup into the glass, before adding a squeeze of lime. Serve with a biodegradable straw and wedge of orange or slightly cheesy umbrella.

A tequila sunrise in any variation must have a gradient of colours down the glass! Don't stir the ingredients before serving and undo your careful hard work!

Rudolph's Red Nose

A take on the classic summer sangria but a little different to mulled wine, warm up those chilly winter nights and thaw those red noses with all your friends and family.

Ingredients
Serves 10-15

- 1 BOTTLE **RED WINE**
- 50 ML **TRIPLE SEC**
- 500 ML **ORANGE JUICE**
- 1.5 L **CRANBERRY JUICE**
- 50 ML **SUGAR SYRUP**
- 200 GR **BROWN SUGAR**
- 1 STICK **CINNAMON**
- ½ TSP **ALMOND EXTRACT**
- SLICED **ORANGE**

LONG

WARMING

SWEET

Method

In a large pan, heat the red wine, triple sec, orange juice, cranberry juice, sugar syrup and cinnamon, except the brown sugar and almond extract until it begins to steam, in about 7 minutes. Take off the heat, add the almond extract and brown sugar and keep stirring until they are dissolved. Serve in latte glasses or mugs.

Keep any of Rudoplh's Red Nose left warm over a low heat for guests to enjoy.

WHITE RUSSIAN CHRISTMAS

A Christmassy take on the classic White Russian, best served in a low light, low key, intimate setting. Father Christmas would need a designated driver or a taxi for delivering presents after one of these!

INGREDIENTS
Serves 1

- 50 ML **VODKA**
- 25 ML **PEPPERMINT SCHNAPPS**
- 25 ML **COFFEE LIQUEUR**
- GARNISH **FLOAT CREAM**

IMPRESS

EXTRAVAGENT

STRONG

METHOD

In a chilled lowball glass add plenty of ice, followed by the vodka, coffee liqueur and peppermint schnapps. Stir gently to combine. For a little extra indulgence, float some fresh cream on top and, if you fancy, serve with a candy cane for decoration.

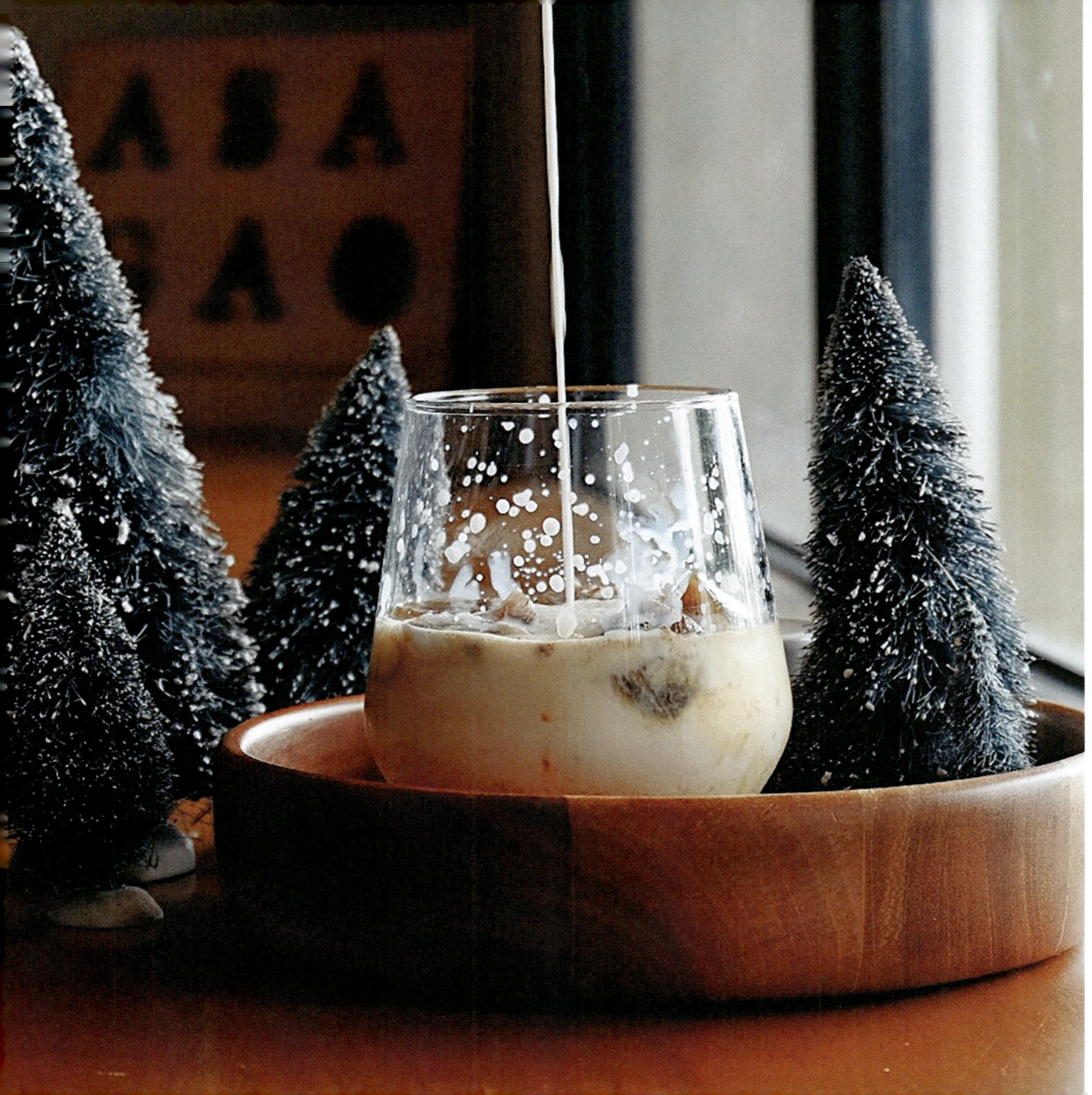

Warm Bourbon Cider

We at Make Me A Cocktail are a fan of the quick to make drinks for a lot of friends, that adds a little something special to a party. Winter parties aren't winter parties without something warming to drink, so why not try something different to mulled wine or gluehwein!

Ingredients
Serves 15-20

- 250 ML **BOURBON WHISKEY**
- 3.5 L **APPLE CIDER**
- 2.5 TSP **GROUND GINGER**
- 2.5 TSP **GROUND NUTMEG**
- 5 TSP **GROUND CINNAMON**

PARTY

LONG

WARMING

Method

In a large pan, combine the apple cider, cinnamon, nutmeg, and ginger. When the liquid is hot but not boiling, remove from heat and add your bourbon whiskey of choice. Stir to distribute the spices and divide this warming winter drink amongst your heat resistant glasses of choice.

Why not make yourself one with a can of warmed cider infused with a sprinkle of spices and a splash of whiskey to serve.

Chocolate Orange Cocktail

Chocolate and orange together. It's a match made in heaven! This decadent, refined cocktail delivers beautifully with those flavours. Get shaking and get serving to get everyone in the Christmas spirit.

Ingredients
Serves 1

- 25 ML **VODKA**
- 25 ML **CRÈME DE CACAO**
- 10 ML **ORANGE JUICE**
- 15 ML **ORANGE SYRUP**

DECADENT

RICH

IMPRESS

Method

First rim a cocktail glass with sugar syrup then dab onto some grated dark chocolate. To make the drink simply shake the vodka, crème de cacao, orange juice and orange syrup in a cocktail shaker with ice, before straining into the rimmed cocktail glass.

Make your own orange syrup by combining 100g caster sugar, with 100ml water and the zest of 1 orange in a pan. Bring to the boil until the sugar dissolves. Leave to cool and you're good to go.

Mulled Pear & Cranberry Punch

There are so many wonderful alternatives to the traditional Mulled Wine at winter, we at Make Me A Cocktail want wintery special occasions to be remembered for being surprisingly different!

Ingredients
Serves 10

- 1 LITRE **PEAR CIDER**
- 150 ML **SLOE GIN**
- 1 LITRE **CRANBERRY JUICE**
- 5 STAR ANISE
- 1 LITRE **PEAR JUICE**
- 2 **VANILLA PODS**
- 2 **CINNAMON STICKS**

PARTY

WARMING

LONG

Method

In a large saucepan add the pear cider, cranberry juice, pear juice, sliced vanilla pods and cinnamon sticks, except for the sloe gin and slowly bring to a simmer. Once simmering, leave for a couple of minutes for the flavours to infuse. Remove from the heat, stir in the sloe gin then serve. Garnish with cinnamon sticks and star anise.

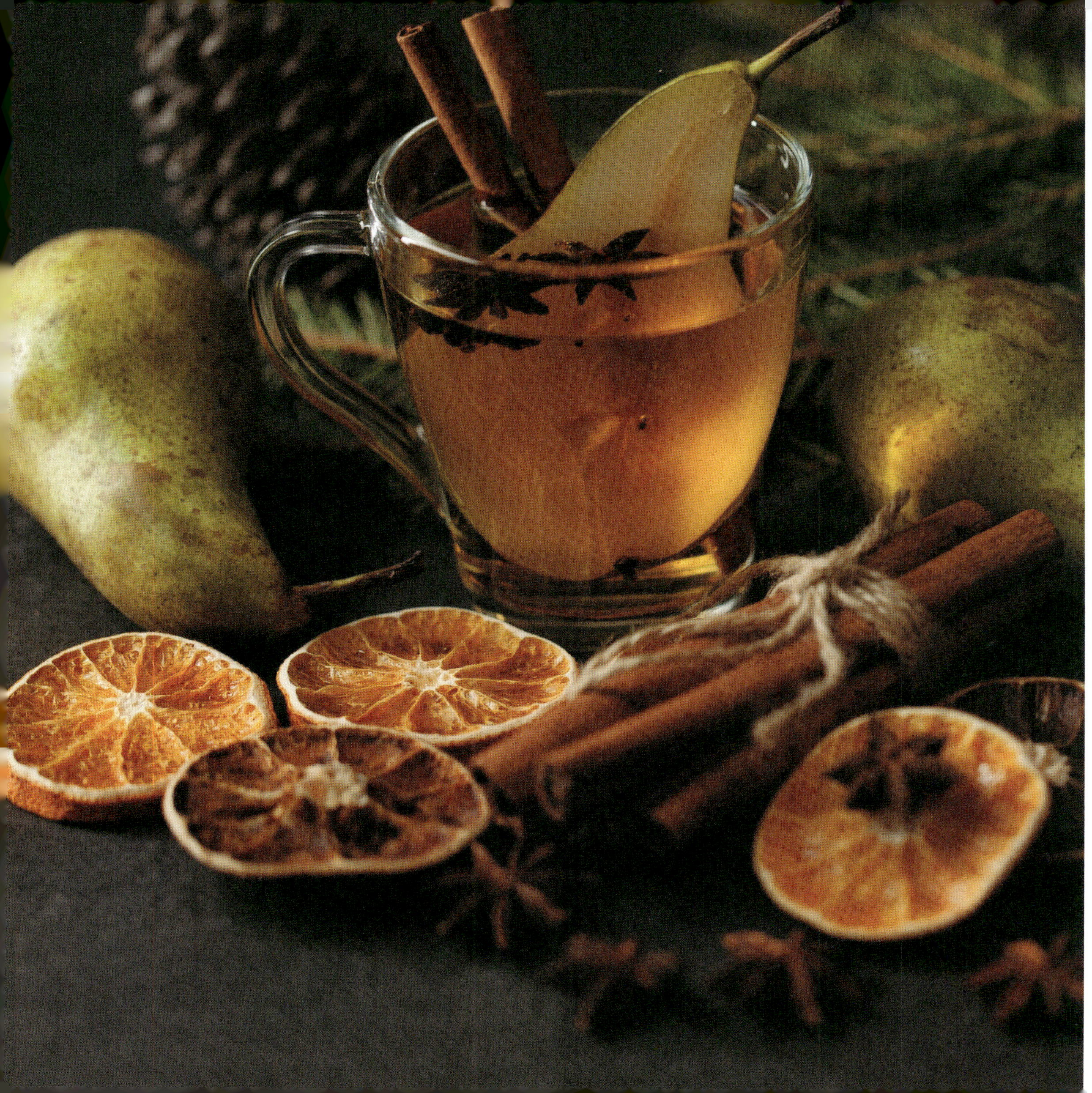

Winter Sidecar

If you're looking to hold and sip a little winter work of art, and fancy something different to the usual vodka, gin and whisky bases, the Winter Sidecar is for you! This cocktail was created in the Make Me a Cocktail online community by Giuseppe Gallo.

Ingredients
Serves 1

- 50 ML **COGNAC**
- 30 ML **BIANCO VERMOUTH**
- 15 ML **CLEMENTINE JUICE**
- TOUCH OF **CINNAMON**

IMPRESS

EXTRAVAGENT

STRONG

Method

Roll the rim of the cocktail glass in water, or for an extra jazz some sugar syrup / orange juice. Once moist roll the rim in the cinnamon to create a cinnamon rim to the glass. Shake the cognac, blanco vermouth and clementine juice in a cocktail shaker with ice, and simply strain into the cocktail glass. Garnish with a sprig of rosemary to awaken the senses.

Can't get hold of clementine juice?
Orange juice will do just fine!

Champagne Comme-il-faut

We're not sure if the linguists among you would agree with the naming of this perfectly balanced non-alcoholic drink, nevertheless it delivers on taste and is perfect for that early Christmas morning for all the family. Let's open those presents!

Ingredients
Serves 4

- 200 ML **PINEAPPLE JUICE**
- 500 ML **GINGER ALE**
- 250 ML **WHITE GRAPE JUICE**

FANCY

NON ALCOHOLIC

SWEET

Method

Pour the white grape juice and pineapple juice into a pitcher half full of ice. Top up with the ginger ale and stir. When serving, serve into champagne flutes and garnish with your favourite fruit - we like a good strawberry on the side.

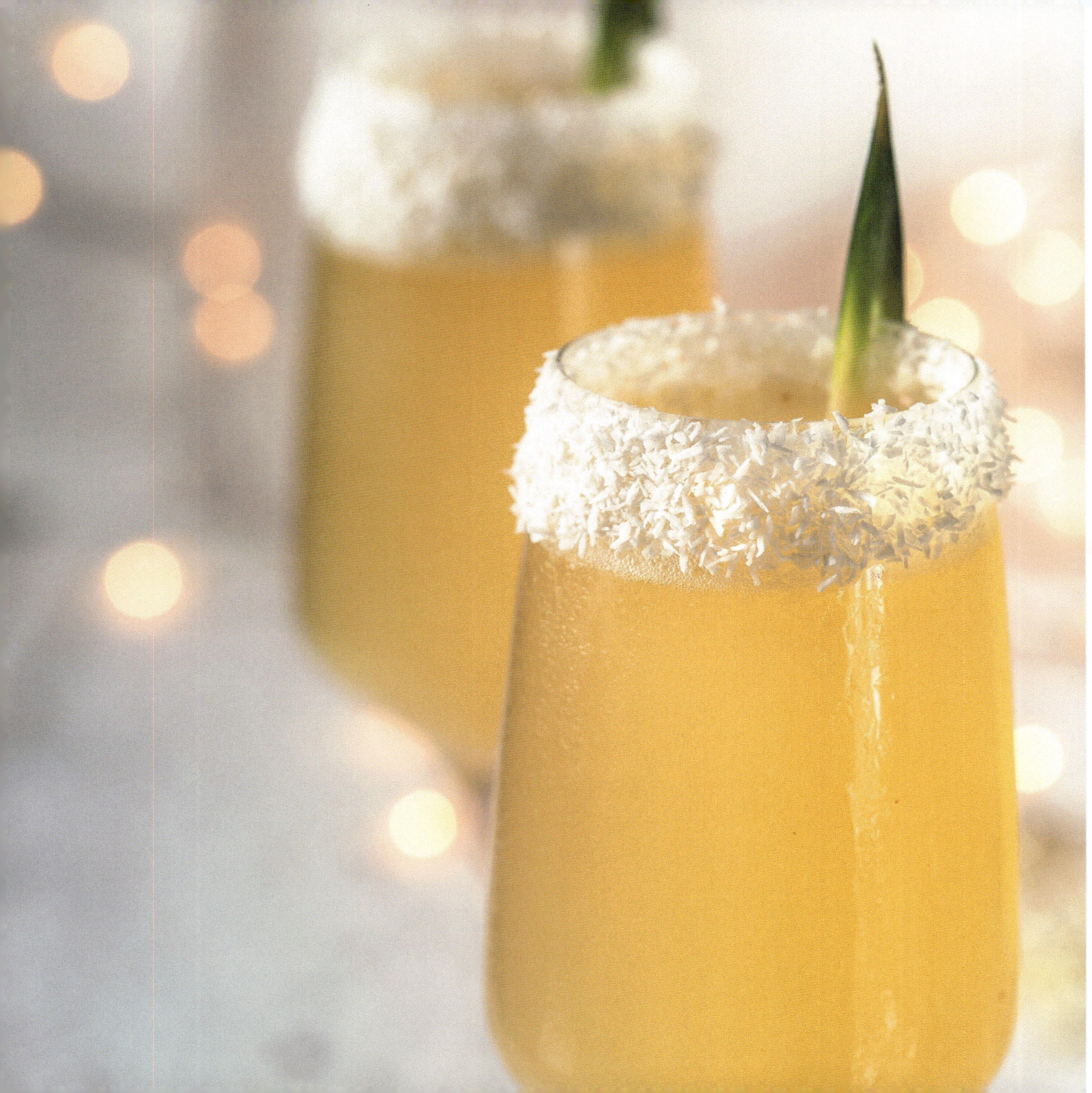

Santa's Nightcap

A sweet and indulgent cocktail created at the Mandarin Oriental in New York City. Perfect for a cold winter nightcap to end an evening or party.

Ingredients
Serves 1

- 50 ML **DARK RUM**
- 15 ML **KAHLUA**
- 25 ML **HALF AND HALF**
- 25 ML **CHOCOLATE CHIP COOKIE SYRUP**

SWEET

EXTRAVAGENT

STRONG

Method

Shake up the dark rum, Kahlua, Half and Half and chocolate chip cookie syrup in a cocktail shaker with ice, before double straining into a sugar rimmed cocktail glass. For added flair at Christmas, garnish with some chocolate pearls and red coloured sugar to rim the glass!

💡

Half and Half is half cream, half milk. Simple to make up if you don't have the exact ingredient!

Winter Pimm's Punch

Punch style cocktails are low maintenance for a party with lots of guests to cater for and still look like you made an effort! We love to serve the Winter Pimm's Punch warmed, in different jars filled with punch and rustic fruit garnishes for a homely, winter party feel. In a hurry to make up more cocktails for guests? This adaptable cocktail tastes great served cold with lots of ice.

Ingredients
Serves 15 - 20

- 500 ML **BRANDY**
- 500 ML **PIMM'S NO. 1**
- 1.5 LITRES **APPLE JUICE**
- HALVED AND SLICED **ORANGE**
- HALVED AND SLICED **APPLE**
- 2 **CINNAMON STICKS**

PARTY

FAST

SIMPLE

Method

If serving warm, combine the brandy, Pimm's, apple juice, orange, apple and cinnamon in a large pan, heat but do not let it boil or simmer. Then, combine all ingredients in a sturdy pitcher, stir and serve. If serving cold, combine all ingredients into a pitcher or punch bowl with lots of ice and stir well before serving. Delicious!

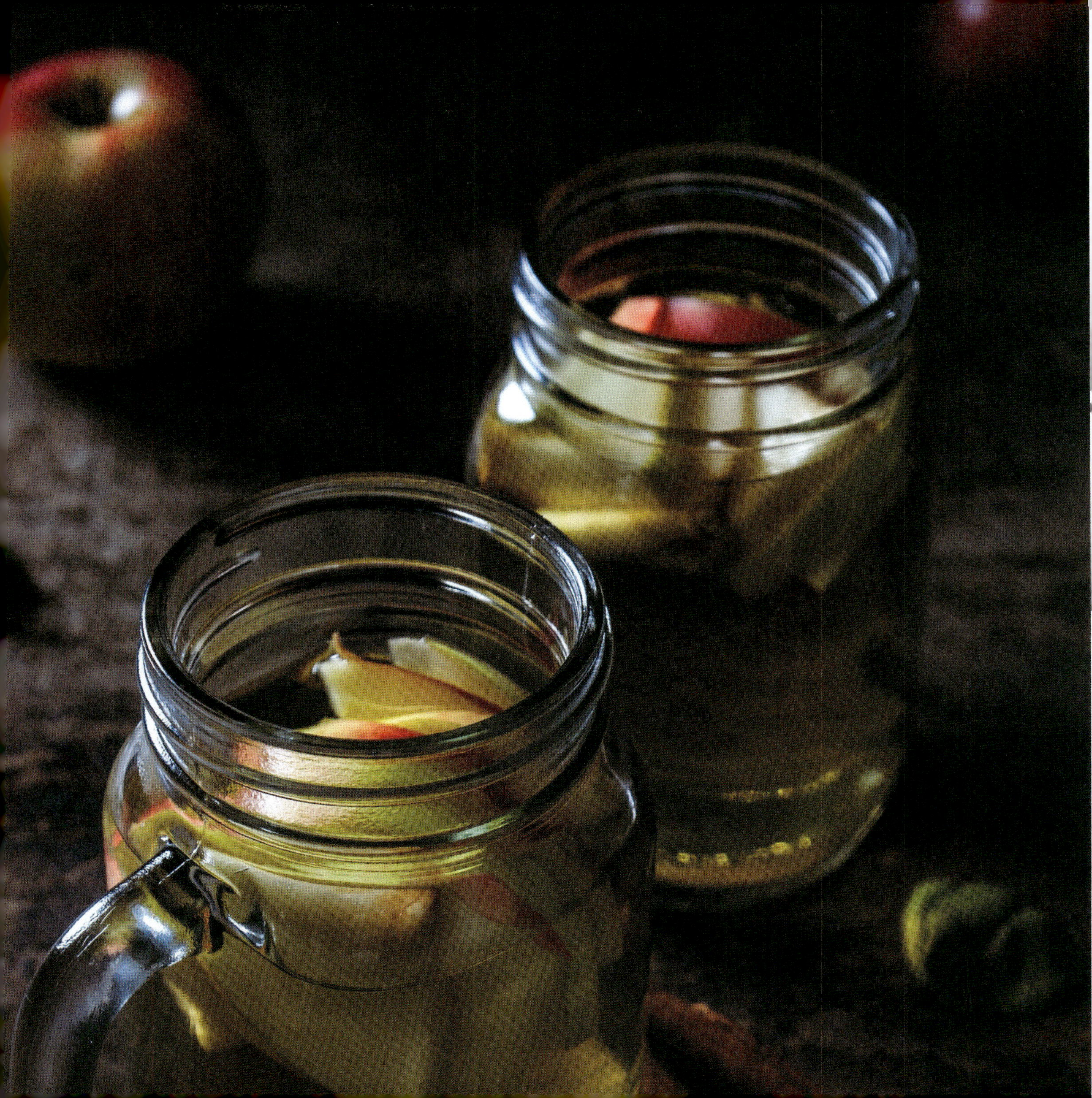

Christmas Cosmopolitan

Loved the world over, this Christmas take on the classic Cosmopolitan keeps the spirit of the original drink true, while adding some warming notes from the ginger and gin.

Ingredients
Serves 1

- 40 ML **GIN**
- 40 ML **VODKA**
- 80 ML **CRANBERRY JUICE**
- ½ **LIME**
- 2 SLICES **GINGER**

CLASSIC

IMPRESS

STRONG

Method

In a mixing glass with ice add in a couple of slices of fresh ginger, before pouring in the vodka, gin and cranberry juice. Next add the juice of half a lime and stir to combine and chill, before straining into a chilled cocktail glass.

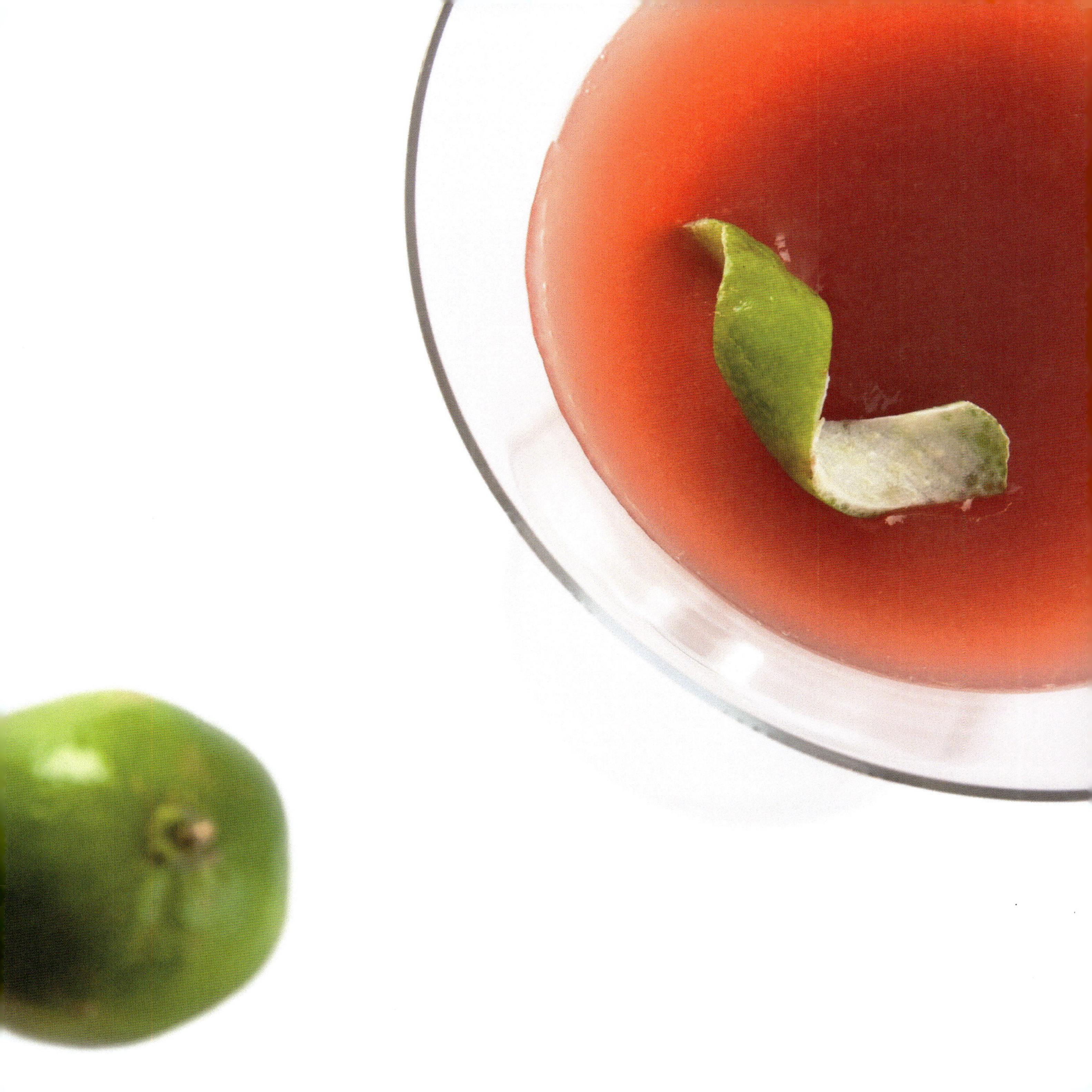

Pimped Up Prosecco

This fruity prosecco-based cocktail makes a great alternative to Bucks Fizz on the morning of Christmas Day!

Ingredients
Serves 1

- **PROSECCO**
- 1 **ORANGE**
- SQUEEZE **POMEGRANATE JUICE**
- SPLASH **ELDERFLOWER CORDIAL**
- ½ **PASSIONFRUIT**
- ½ **LIME**
- ¼ **GRAPEFRUIT**

IMPRESS

DECADENT

LONG

Method

Squeeze the orange, lime, grapefruit and passionfruit, add the pomegranate juice and elderflower cordial into a cocktail shaker with ice. Shake for 15-20 seconds or until the outside of the cocktail shaker gets too cold. Evenly distribute the fruit mixture between two or three champagne flutes. Top up each flute with prosecco, garnish and serve.

For a non-alcoholic alternative, swap the prosecco for lemonade. For extra indulgence, swap prosecco with Champagne.

Christmas Snowball

No, this isn't made by throwing snowballs around in the kitchen - although that would be fun (and recommended), this simple 3 ingredient cocktail hits the spot without hitting a massive alcoholic punch.

Ingredients
Serves 1

- 25 ML **ADVOCAAT**
- 25 ML **GINGER SYRUP**
- TOP UP **BABYCHAM**

WARMING

SWEET

LIGHT

Method

Rim the highball glass with water and then sugar (or for added flair we suggest Christmas sprinkles). Into a cocktail shaker with ice, add the ginger syrup with advocaat and shake for 10-15 seconds. Strain into the ice filled highball glass and top up with the Babycham.

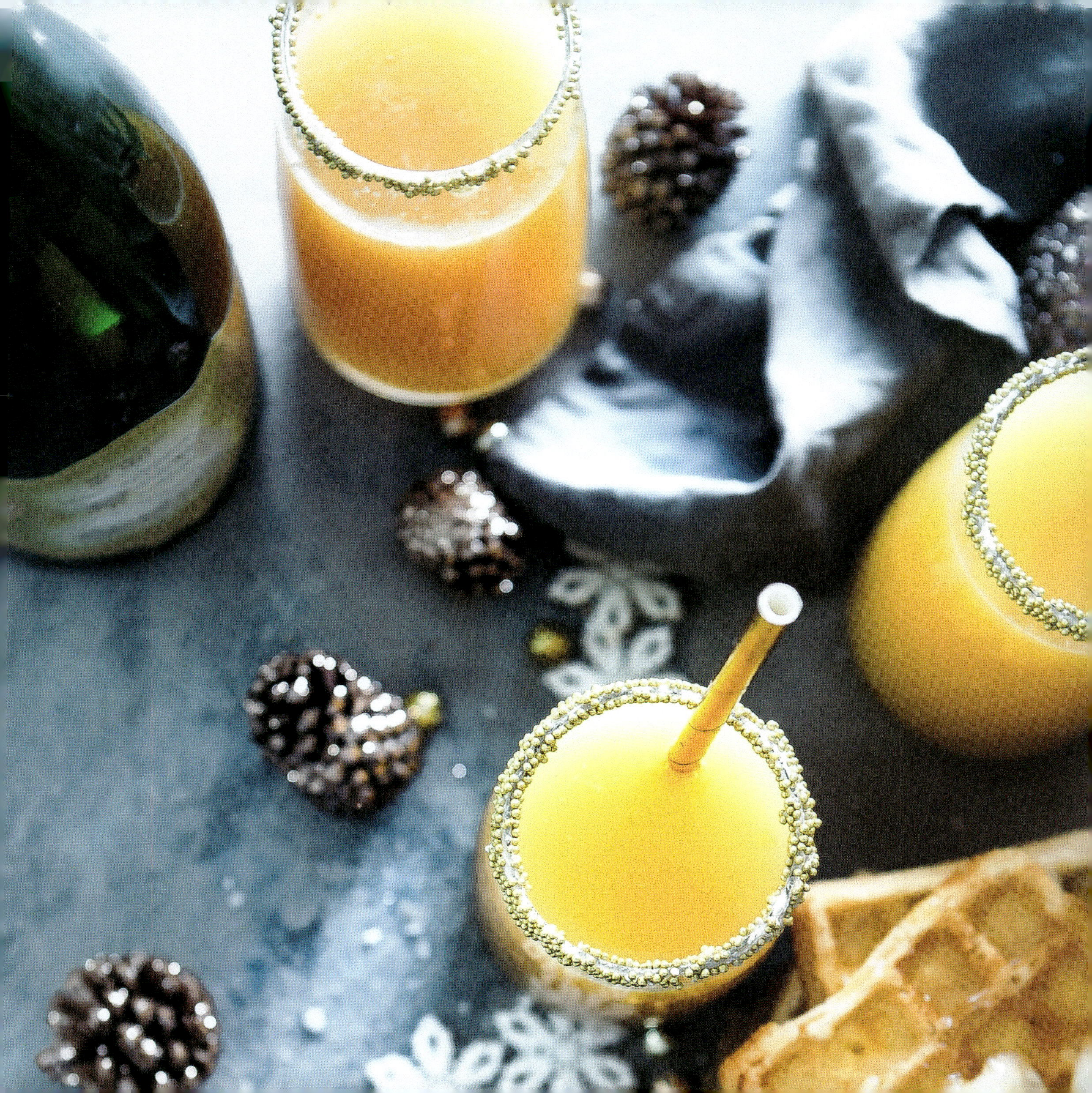

Glogg

A traditional Swedish take on Mulled Wine, Glogg is an essential part of any lead up to Christmas in Sweden. We've heard rumours that Glogg parties are thrown almost every weekend during Advent. Swedish fans of Make Me A Cocktail, we accept your invitation!

Ingredients
Serves 6

- 750 ML **RED WINE**
- 85 G **SUGAR**
- 2 SLICES **GINGER**
- 1 **CINNAMON STICK**
- 15 **CLOVES**
- 6 **CARDAMOM PODS**

PARTY

WARMING

SPICE

Method

Simply add the red wine, sugar, ginger, cinnamon stick, cloves and cardamom into a suitable large saucepan and heat slowly until the flavours have all infused. Do not let the mixture boil. Ladle into quirky Christmas mugs or latte glasses, garnish with orange peel if you like and enjoy!

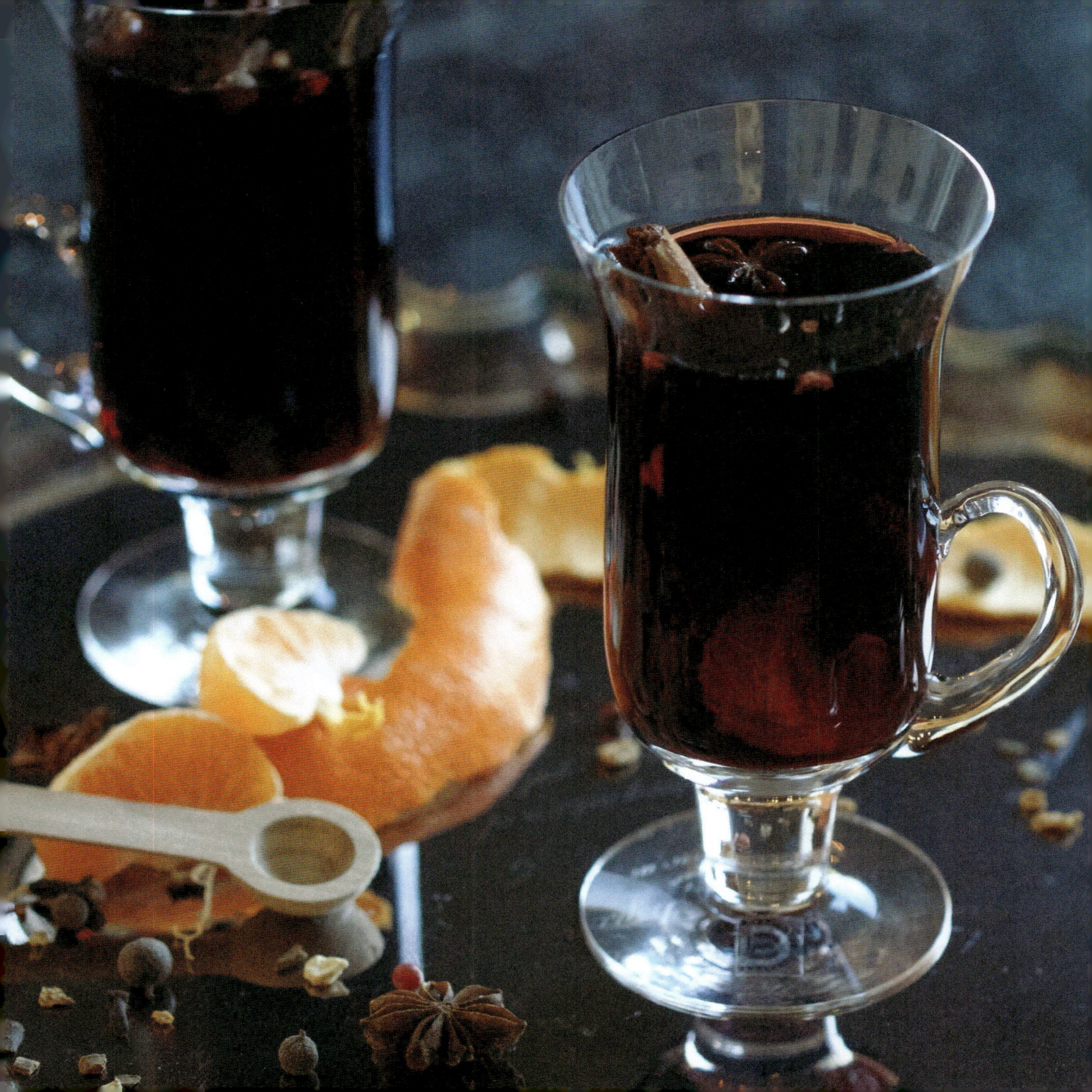

Baby Bellini

This delicious spin off from the 1930's Bellini, is a virgin version of that classic peach and Champagne delight. Let the kids feel special on Christmas morning with one of these, or the adults who might have enjoyed Christmas Eve a little too much…

Ingredients
Serves 1

- 50 ML **PEACH JUICE**
- 25 ML **LEMON JUICE**
- TOP UP **SPARKLING APPLE JUICE**
- SLICE **PEACH**

BRUNCH

NON ALCOHOLIC

SIMPLE

Method

Pour the peach juice and lemon juice into a chilled champagne flute and stir well. Top up the glass with the sparkling apple juice, stir gently to combine, garnish with a peach slice and give to the eagerly awaiting (or hungover!) family member. Delicious.

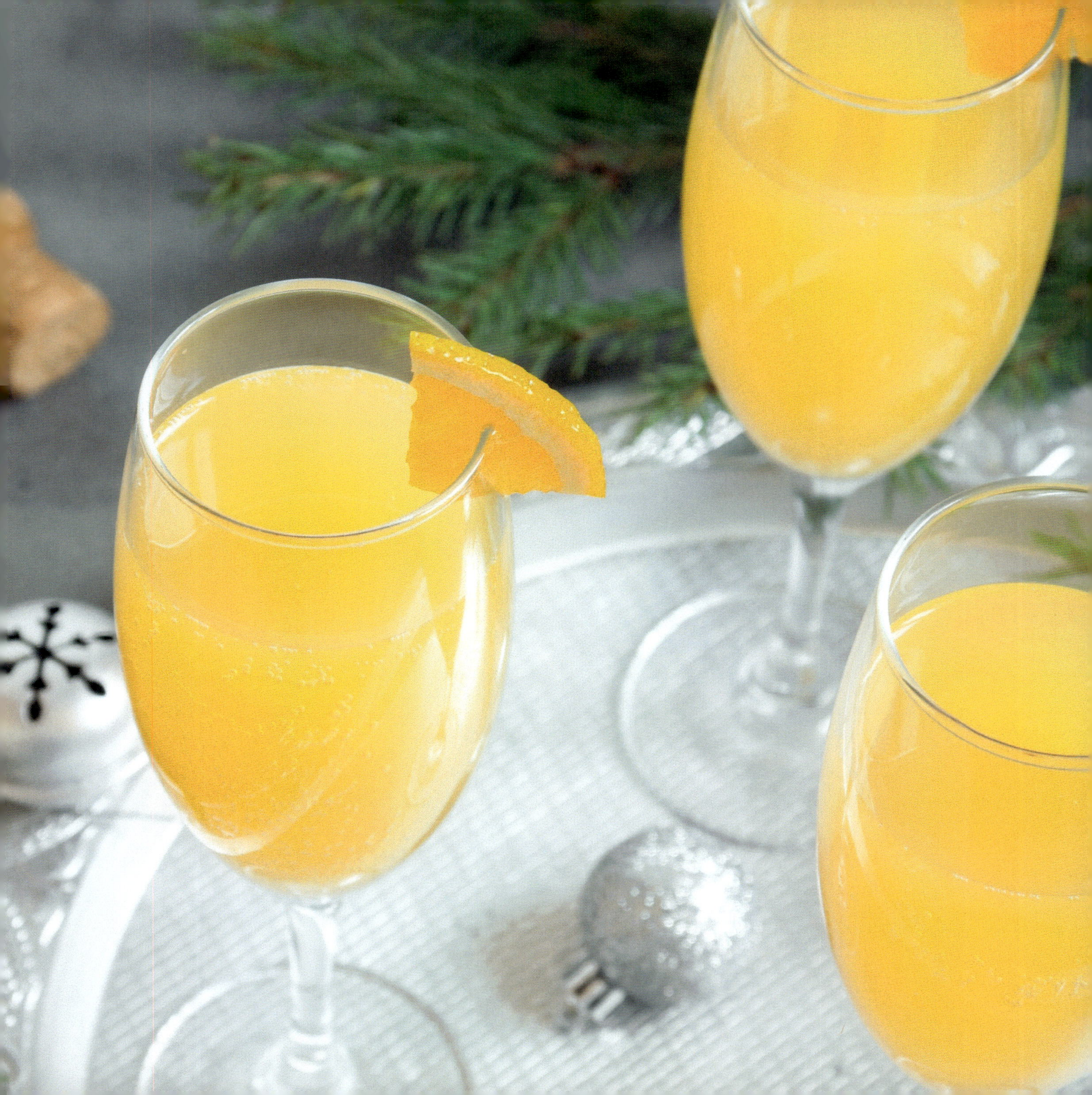

Winter Whiskey Sour

Need a sophisticated end to a dinner party or an evening with friends on a cold winter night? The heat of the whiskey and the ice-cold citrus and sweetness is a taste sensation at the end of a night!

Ingredients
Serves 1

- 50 ML **BOURBON WHISKEY**
- 1 TBSP **ORANGE JUICE**
- 1 TBSP **LEMON JUICE**
- ½ TBSP **SUGAR SYRUP**
- SLICE **ORANGE PEEL**

SIMPLE

SOPHISTICATED

EXTRAVAGENT

Method

Fill a glass with crushed ice to let it cool. Add the bourbon whiskey, sugar syrup, orange juice and lemon juice into a cocktail shaker with ice and shake hard. Strain into the chilled glass. Garnish with a slice of orange peel and serve.

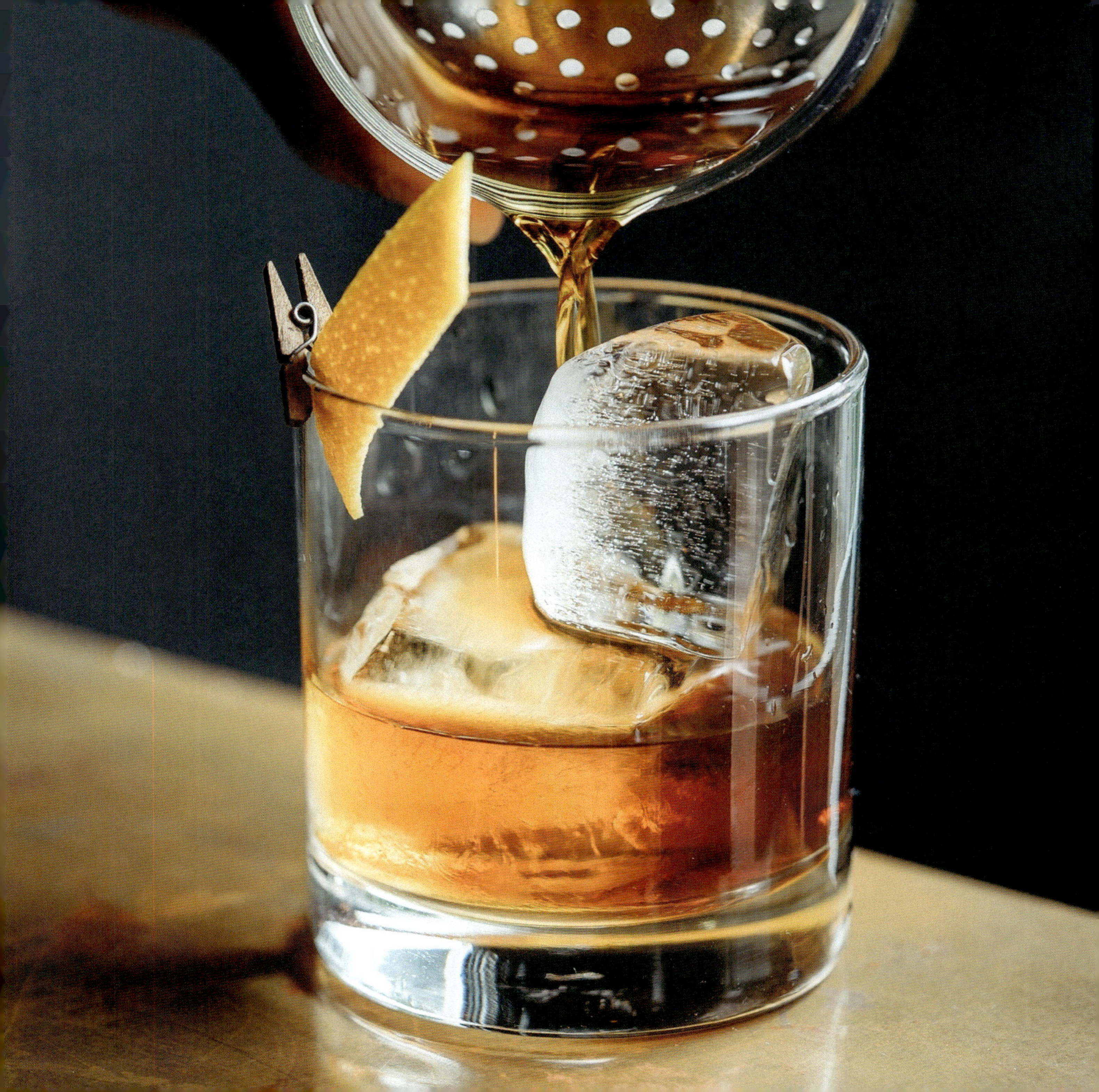

The North Pole

Legend has it this decadent Christmas cocktail fires up Saint Nicholas before he prepares himself for the Christmas season… or at least we like to think it does! This an extremely indulgent cocktail, so enjoy without thinking about the calories!

Ingredients
Serves 1

- 25 ML **KAHLUA**
- 50 ML **VODKA**
- 15 ML **SUGAR SYRUP**
- 60 ML **DOUBLE CREAM**
- 2 TBSP **CHOCOLATE SYRUP**
- ½ TSP **VANILLA ESSENCE**
- ¼ TSP **GROUND GINGER**

SWEET

STRONG

IMPRESS

Method

In a cocktail shaker with ice combine the vodka, Kahlua, chocolate syrup, vanilla essence, sugar syrup and ginger. Shake hard until the outside of the cocktail shaker becomes frosted. Strain into a chilled lowball glass before topping up with the cream.

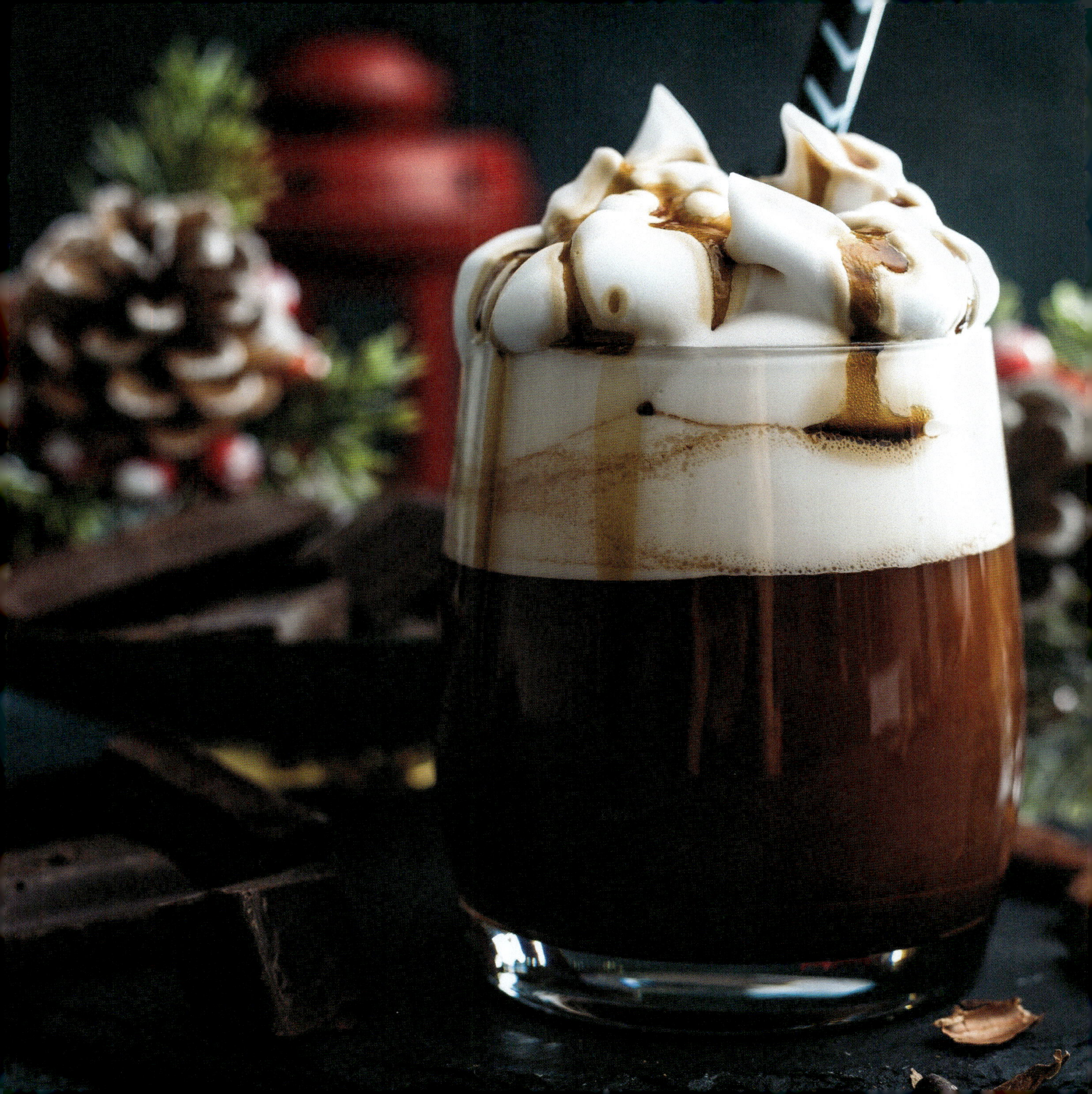

Hot Peppermint Patty

Looking for an alternative after-dinner drink or finding your inner hygge in winter, the Hot Peppermint Patty takes a traditional hot chocolate and gives it a minty, alcoholic twist. Bliss on a cold winter's night.

Ingredients
Serves 1

- 25 ML **PEPPERMINT SCHNAPPS**
- 1 TSP **CRÈME DE MENTHE**
- 12.5 ML **CRÈME DE CACAO DARK**
- 125 ML **HOT CHOCOLATE**
- 50 ML **WHIPPED CREAM**
- GARNISH **CHOCOLATE SHAVINGS**

WARMING

INDULGENT

COMFORT

Method

First make your hot chocolate base as normal with your favourite choice of hot chocolate. Once prepared, add the Peppermint Schnapps, the Dark Crème de Cacao, and a teaspoon of Crème de Menthe.

Fill any available space (or lack of) with whipped cream and sprinkle some chocolate shavings (or marshmallows) on top as a finishing touch. Enjoy immediately while warm!

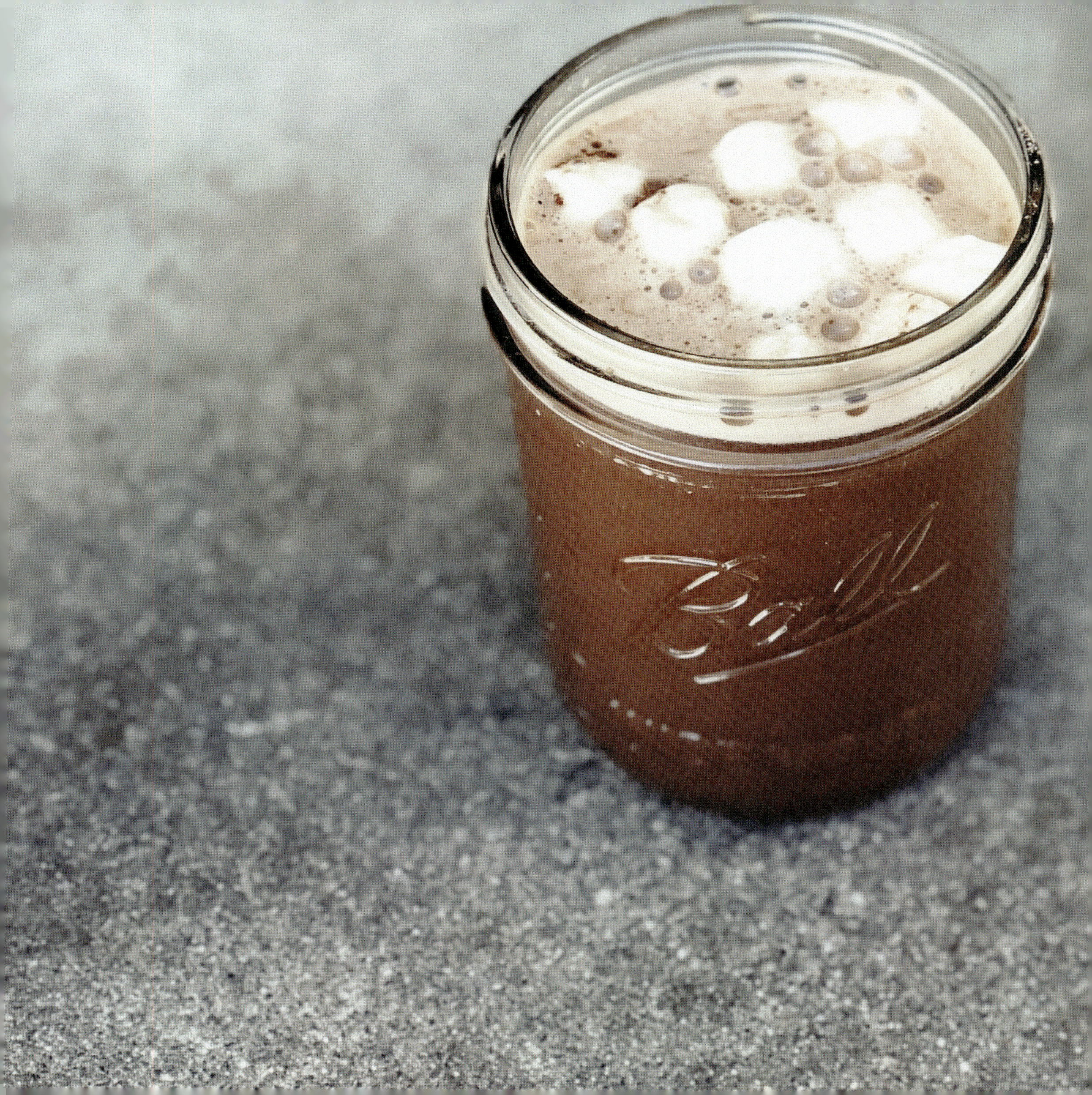
Ball

Snowball

When you think of a classic cocktail for winter, the Snowball tops the list! This classic winter warmer cocktail is made with equal parts advocaat, lemonade and lime juice. Try not to adapt the recipe too far from the classic white colour of a Snowball, because well, we all know not to eat yellow snow!

Ingredients
Serves 1

- 25 ML **ADVOCAAT**
- 25 ML **LEMONADE**
- 25 ML **LIME JUICE**
- GARNISH **CINNAMON**

SIMPLE

FAST

IMPRESS

Method

Shake the lime juice and advocaat together in a cocktail shaker with ice. Strain into the desired glass and top up with lemonade. Garnish with a little grated cinnamon to complete.

Make the snowball a longer drink by serving in a tall glass with lots of ice!

BRANDY EGGNOG

Love it or hate it, we had to include the classic Christmas cocktail Eggnog. Make Me A Cocktail like to find recipes that take a little spin on a classic, and our favourite by far is the rich, aroma filled Brandy Eggnog.

INGREDIENTS
Serves 1

- 25 ML **BRANDY**
- 35 ML **MILK**
- 15 ML **SUGAR SYRUP**
- 1 **EGG YOLK**

SIMPLE

RICH

SWEET

METHOD

There's nothing complicated or extravagant about this recipe; simply add the brandy, milk, sugar syrup and egg yolk into a cocktail shaker with ice and give it a good hard shake for 10-15 seconds. Strain into a nice lowball glass with a few ice cubes, sprinkle a touch of ground cinnamon if you desire and serve.

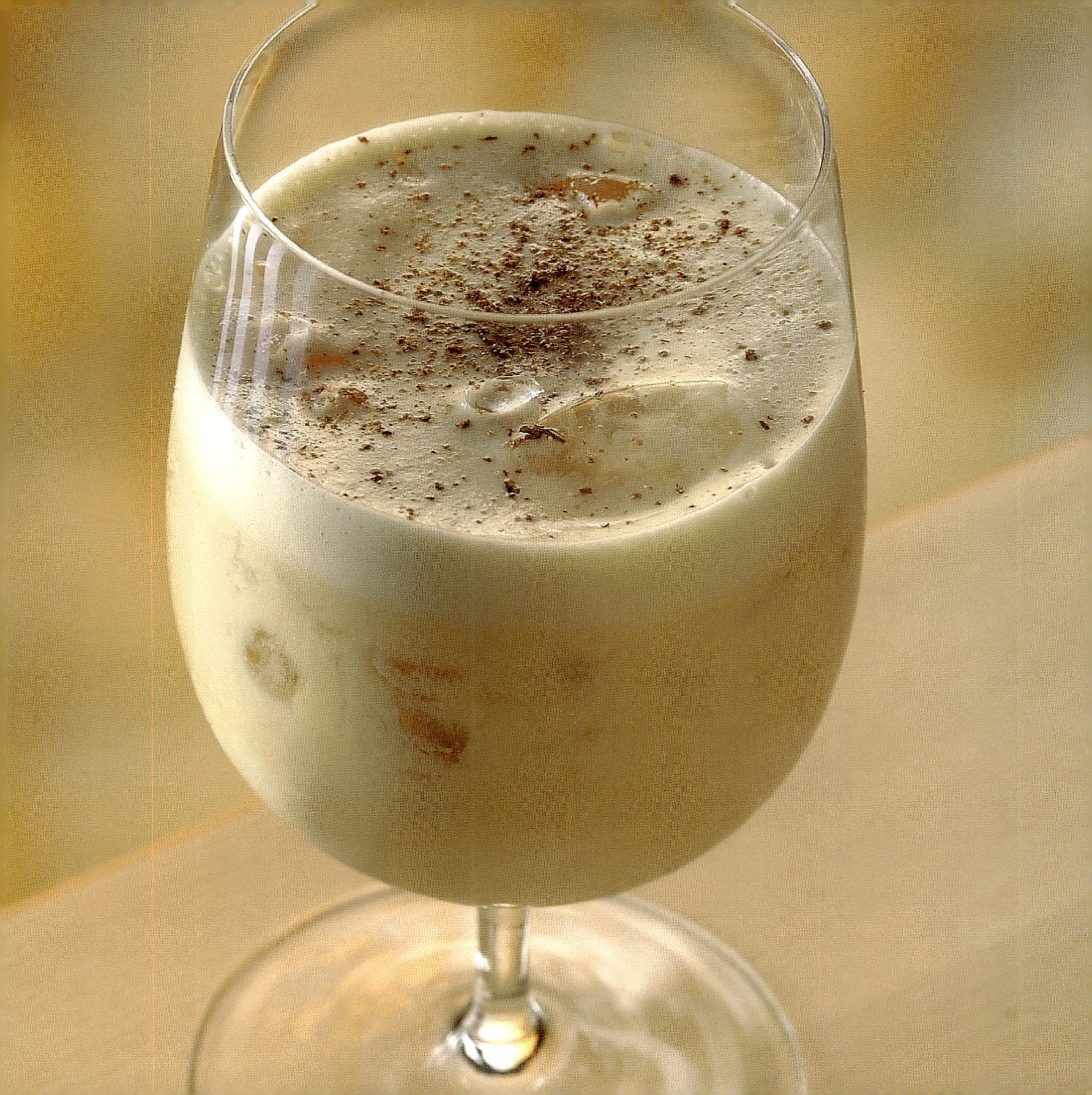

CHRISTMAS PUDDING SOUR

Got some leftover Christmas pudding that no-one managed to fit in? No problem, we've got the perfect use in this tasty take on the classic sour. The Christmas Pudding Sour never disappoints our gin loving friends and family at Christmas!

INGREDIENTS
Serves 1

- 50 ML **GIN**
- 25 G **CHRISTMAS PUDDING**
- 20 ML **LEMON JUICE**
- 15 ML **SUGAR SYRUP**
- 1 EGG **WHITE**

RICH

SOUR

IMPRESS

METHOD

You'll need to extract as much flavour from the Christmas pudding as you can before making your cocktail. Infuse the gin with the Christmas pudding for at least 30 minutes, ideally a couple of hours.

Once infused, simply add the gin, lemon juice, sugar syrup and egg white into a cocktail shaker with ice, shake hard for 10-15 seconds before straining into an ice filled lowball glass. Serve with an orange peel twist and enjoy.

The longer you leave the infusion the stronger that Christmas flavour will be, make a large batch of Pudding infused gin and store.

CHRISTMAS PUNCH

Perfect punch for a Christmas party! The Pomegranate and Cranberry Juice gives it a fruity festive flavour, while Vodka and Cointreau will warm the guests when they arrive out of the frosty weather.

INGREDIENTS
Serves 10

- 200 ML **VODKA**
- 200 ML **COINTREAU**
- 200 ML **CRANBERRY JUICE**
- 200 ML **LEMON JUICE**
- 400 ML **POMEGRANATE JUICE**
- 100 ML **SUGAR SYRUP**
- 100 ML **SODA WATER**
- GARNISH **CRANBERRIES AND LEMON**

PARTY

SWEET

LONG

METHOD

Simply add all the ingredients into a suitably large festive bowl, adding the soda water last, before giving it a quick stir and taste. Garnish with cranberries and lemon slices, and give your guests lowball glasses filled with ice so they can help themselves and go back for more.

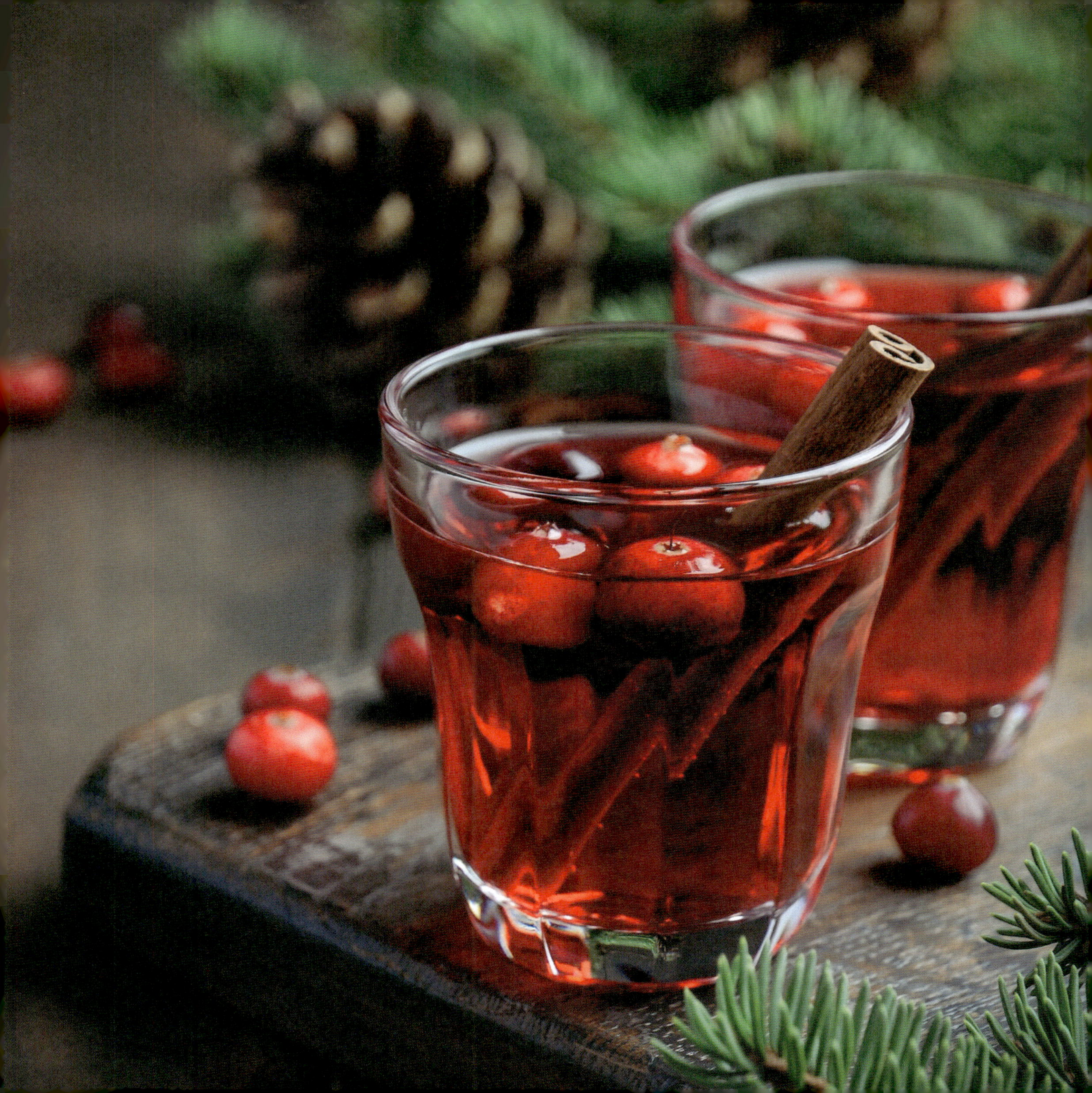

CHRISTMAS COFFEE

Taking the classic Irish coffee and infusing with some wonderful Christmas flavours, the Christmas Coffee is a real treat with a real kick to serve at a relaxed Christmas breakfast, making it a twist on your morning tradition.

INGREDIENTS
Serves 1

- 15 ML **COINTREAU**
- 15 ML **CRÈME DE CACAO**
- 20 ML **IRISH WHISKEY**
- 85 ML **COFFEE**

STRONG

SIMPLE

WARMING

METHOD

Make up your coffee as you like it, before gently pouring in the Cointreau, Crème-de-Cacao and Irish Whiskey. Serve as is, or add milk or cream to personal taste.

Add a bit of Cointreau to some full fat milk, froth up to lather and gently pour on top of the drink.

Hot Buttered Rum

You won't get far through Christmas without being offered some warm drink to socialize and celebrate through the cold nights. The classic Hot Buttered Rum brings the feelings of the festive period to life with its rich rum-based deliciousness.

Ingredients
Serves 1

- 50 ML **DARK RUM**
- 1 TSP **BROWN SUGAR**
- 1 TSP **BUTTER**
- ¼ TSP **GROUND NUTMEG**
- ¼ TSP **GROUND CINNAMON**
- 3 DROPS **VANILLA ESSENCE**

WARMING

SPICE

CLASSIC

Method

Add the melted butter, sugar, vanilla essence, nutmeg and cinnamon into the bottom of a tall coffee glass. Mix well then add the dark rum. Top up with boiling water. Give it a good stir to combine, ensuring the sugar is dissolved, before serving while hot.

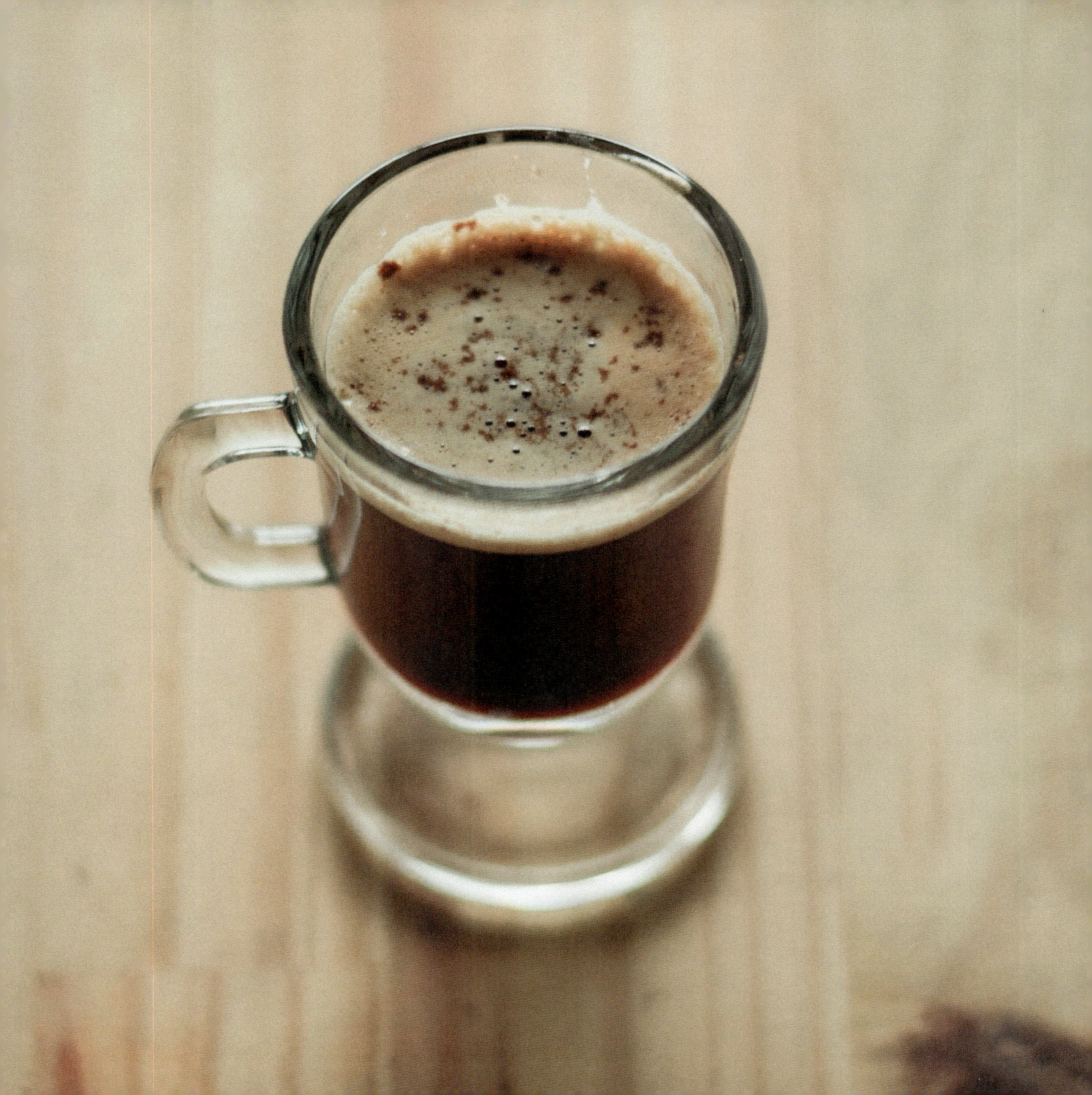

Pumpkin Latte

When we think of winter, we think of hearty vegetables and comfort food. This is an alternative, thick, rich latte, a perfect non-alcoholic alternative to spice up a cold winter's day.

Ingredients
Serves 3

- 400 ML **MILK**
- 250 ML **COFFEE**
- 100 G **PUMPKIN PUREE**
- 3 TBSP **BROWN SUGAR**
- ¼ TSP **GROUND CINNAMON**
- GARNISH **WHIPPED CREAM**

SWEET

NON ALCOHOLIC

WARMING

Method

In a large pan, mix the milk, pumpkin puree, sugar and ground cinnamon. Heat gently, whisking constantly until the mixture just reaches boiling point. Transfer the mixture to three Irish coffee glasses. To garnish, top the glasses with whipped cream and a dusting of cinnamon sugar.

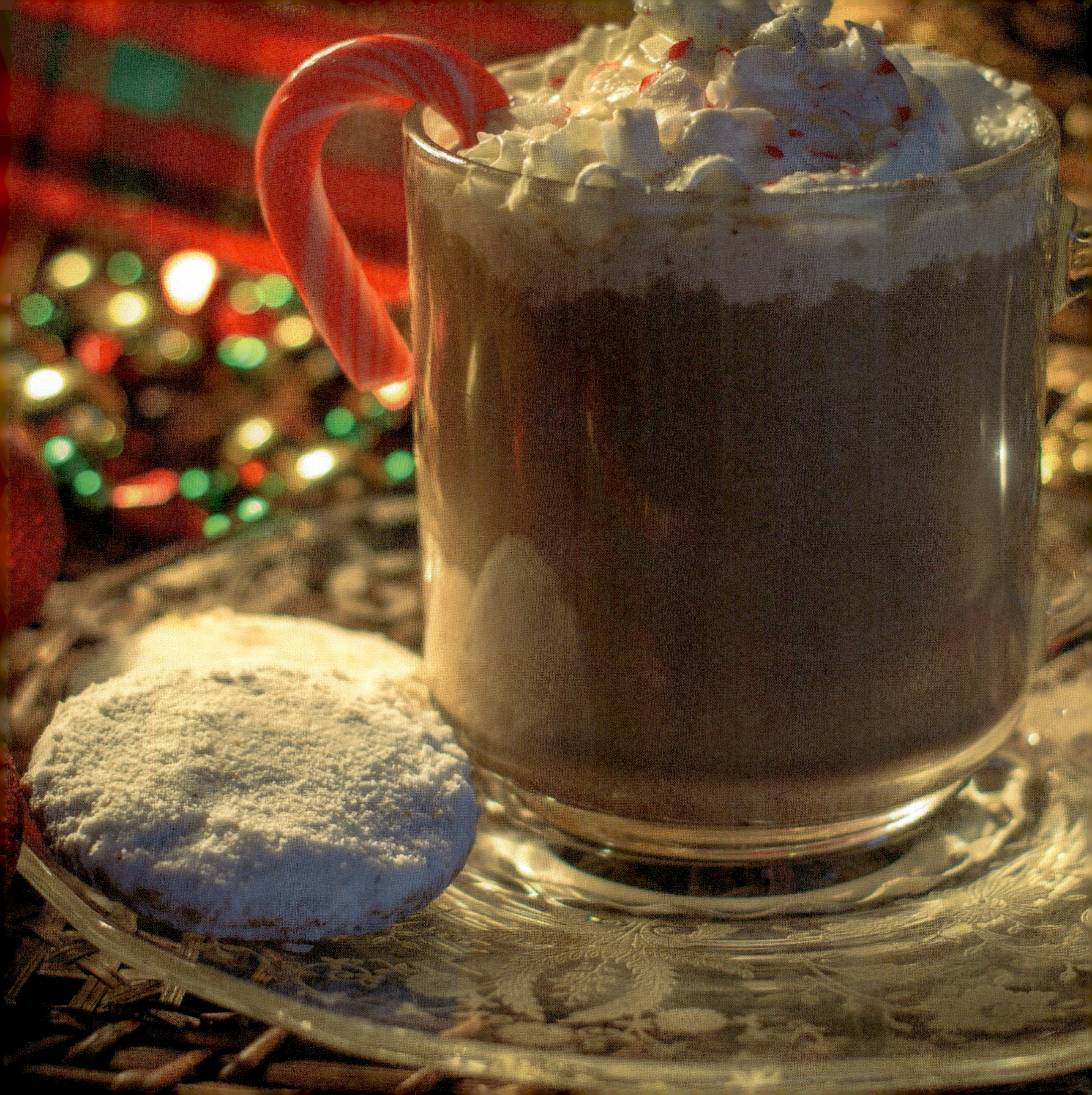

Martin's Rum

We recommend multiplying the recipe and making a batch of this citrussy, warming cocktail and serving to friends with a suitably bad Christmas jumper on.

Ingredients
Serves 1

- 50 ML **151-PROOF RUM**
- 35 ML **DARK RUM**
- 25 ML **SUGAR SYRUP**
- 50 ML **ORANGE JUICE**
- 35 ML **LEMON JUICE**
- 25 ML **LIME JUICE**

LONG

WARMING

CITRUS

Method

With your Christmas knit on get a suitable saucepan and add the 151 Proof Rum, dark rum, sugar syrup, and the three juices. Heat up slowly, ensuring the sugar has dissolved and flavours bought together before serving. Simply pour into an Irish coffee glass and let the warm notes slide down.

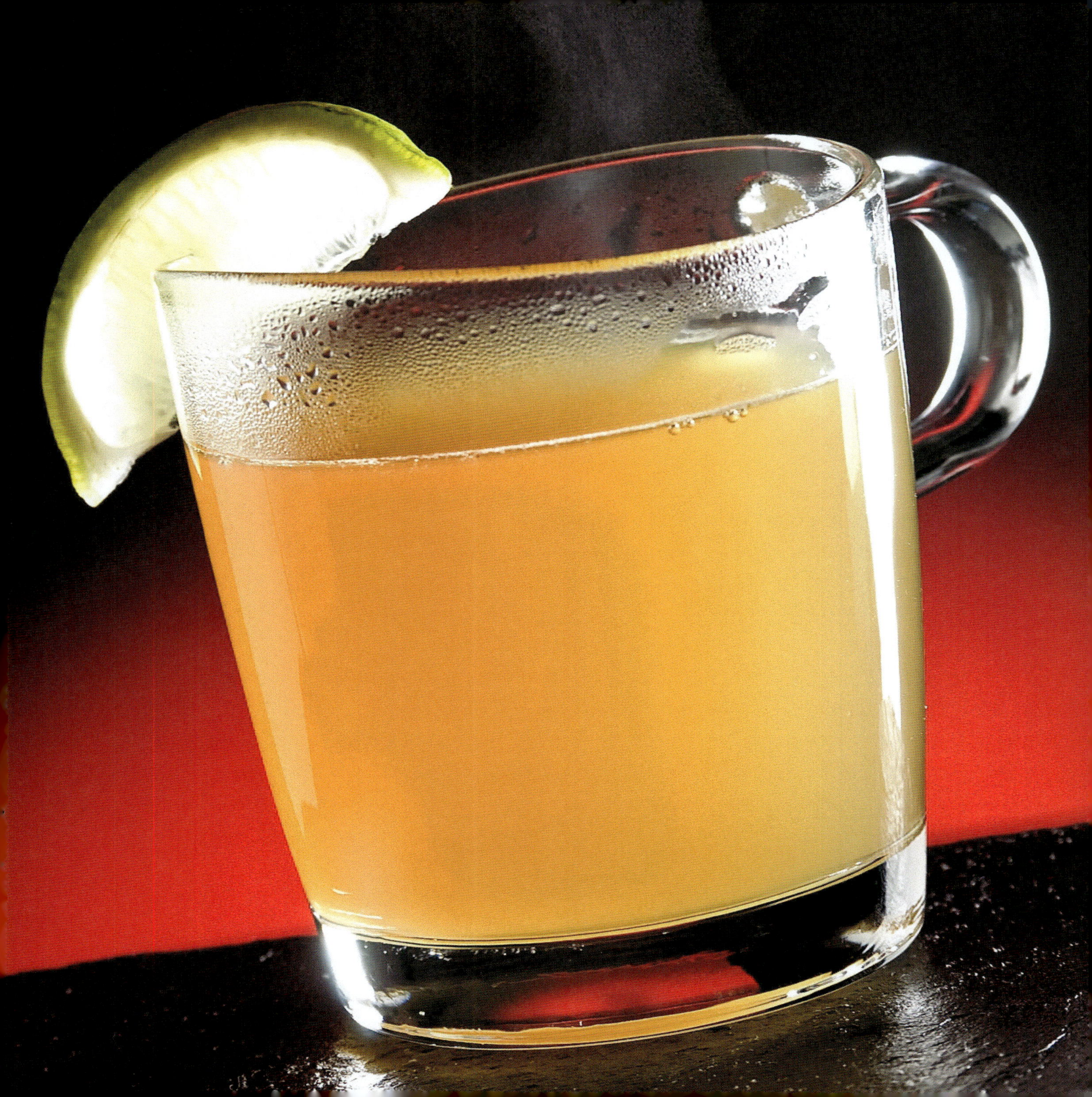

Mocha Eggnog Latte

The wonderful community at Make Me A Cocktail have taken the Christmas drink Eggnog and combined it with coffee and chocolate flavours for a delicious yet simple twist to this classic.

Ingredients
Serves 1

- 25 ML **ESPRESSO COFFEE**
- 25 ML **CHOCOLATE SYRUP**
- TOP UP **EGGNOG**
- GARNISH **WHIPPED CREAM**

SIMPLE

WARMING

SWEET

Method

Combine the chocolate syrup and espresso in an Irish coffee glass. Top up the glass with eggnog and finish with whipped cream and a little grated nutmeg if you like.

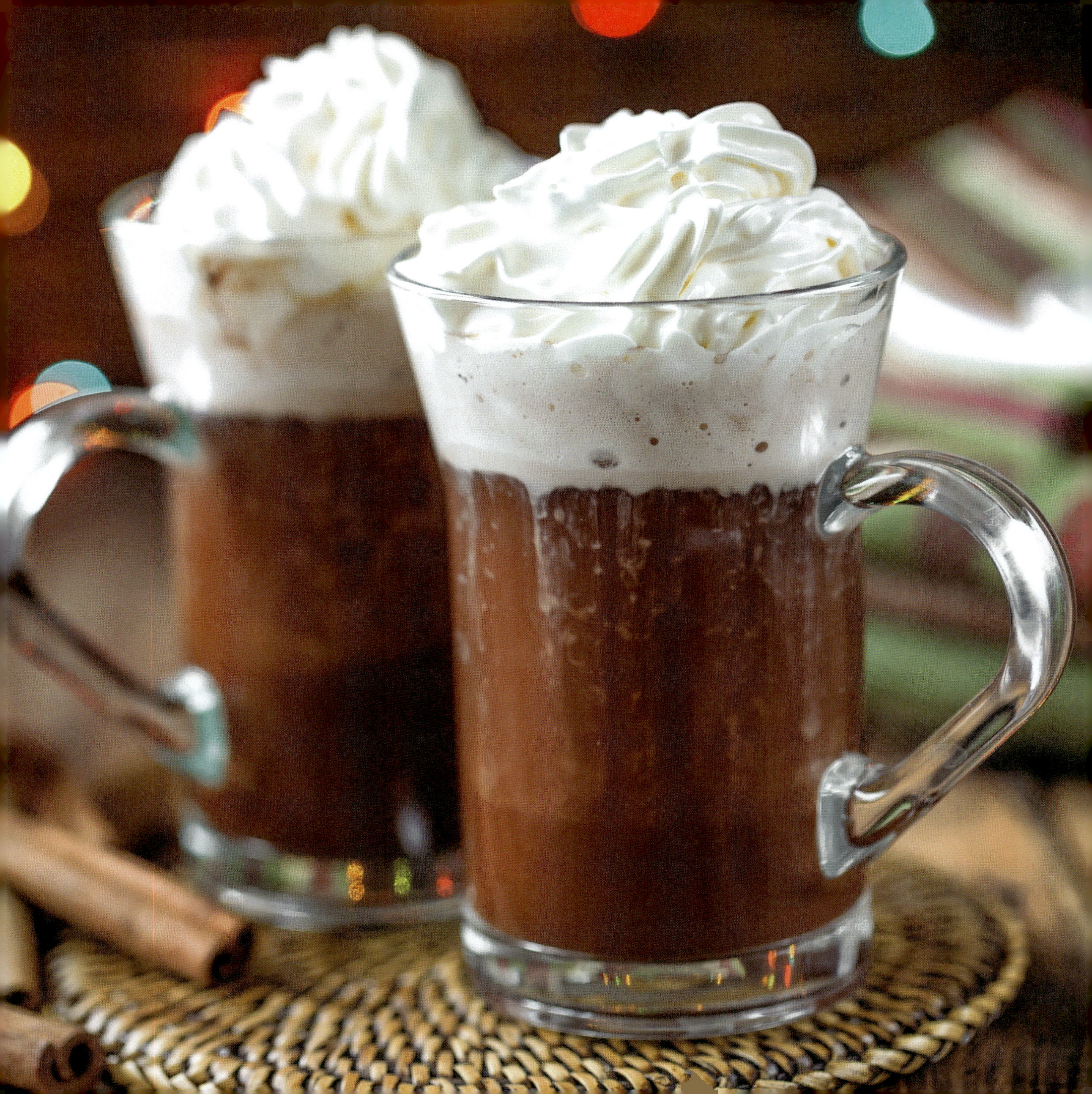

Mimosa

I'm not sure about you, but Christmas wouldn't be Christmas without a cheeky champagne flute of Mimosa in the morning to begin Christmas Day celebrations in style. The classic Mimosa we all know and love; pop open a bottle of champagne in the morning to the delights of friends and family.

Ingredients
Serves 1

- 75 ML **ORANGE JUICE**
- 75 ML **CHAMPAGNE**

SIMPLE

CLASSIC

IMPRESS

Method

Add in 75ml of orange juice to the bottom of a champagne flute before topping up with chilled champagne. Serve with a slice of orange.

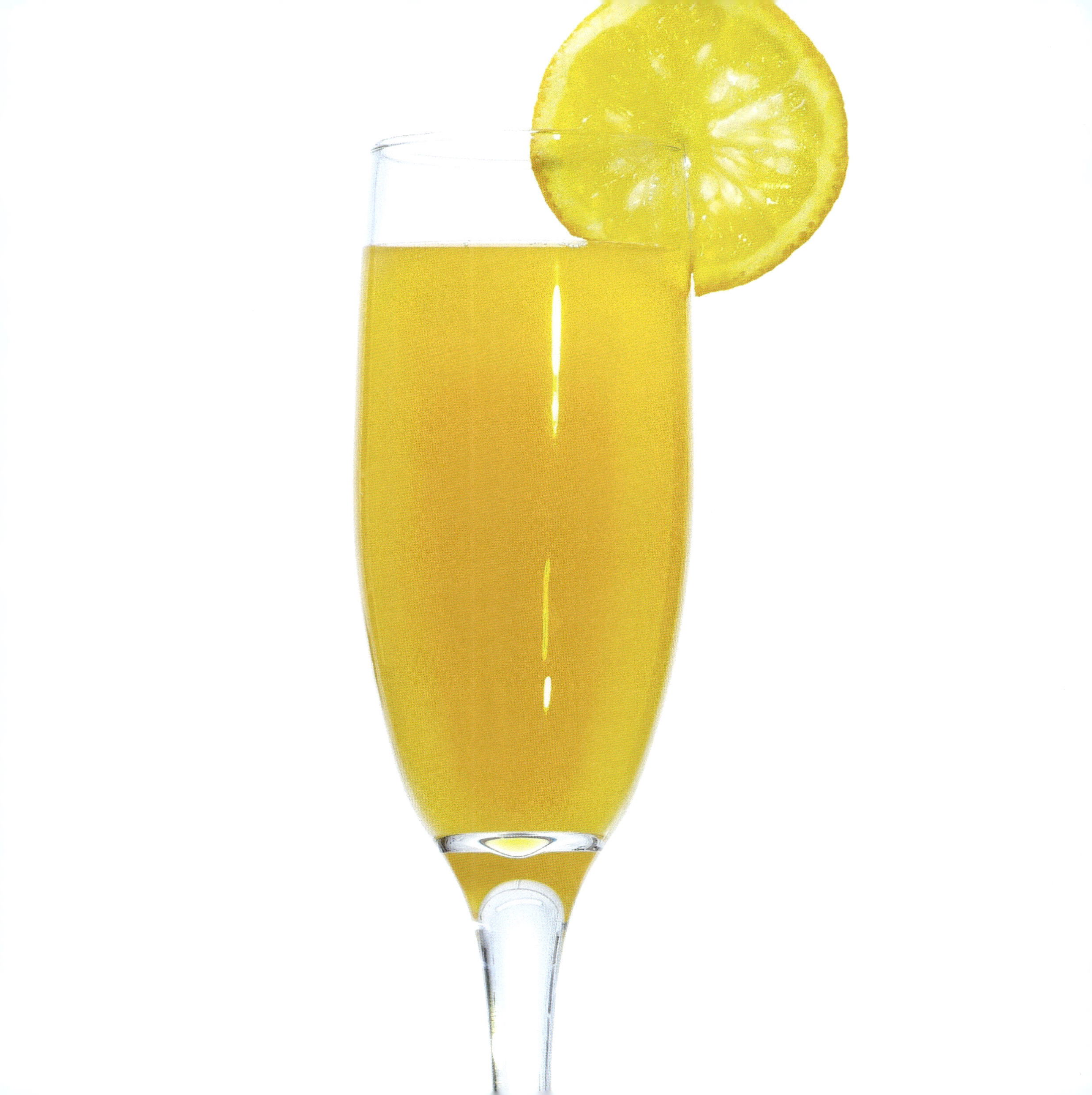

Christmas Baubles

Created at one of the Make Me A Cocktail's family Christmas parties, this has become a tradition at Christmas to enjoy amongst friends and family that we wanted to share with fellow cocktail enthusiasts

Ingredients
Serves 1

- 10 ML **CRANBERRY LIQUEUR**
- 150 ML **PROSECCO OR CHAMPAGNE**
- 5 **FROZEN CRANBERRIES**
- GARNISH **EDIBLE GLITTER**

SIMPLE

CLASSIC

IMPRESS

Method

In the bottom of a champagne glass add the frozen cranberries and cranberry liqueur. Slowly top up with your favourite prosecco or champagne, taking care not to let the bubbles over fizz. To serve, sprinkle a little edible glitter into the glass, the bubbles in the champagne flute glitter like the Christmas baubles against the lights on your tree!

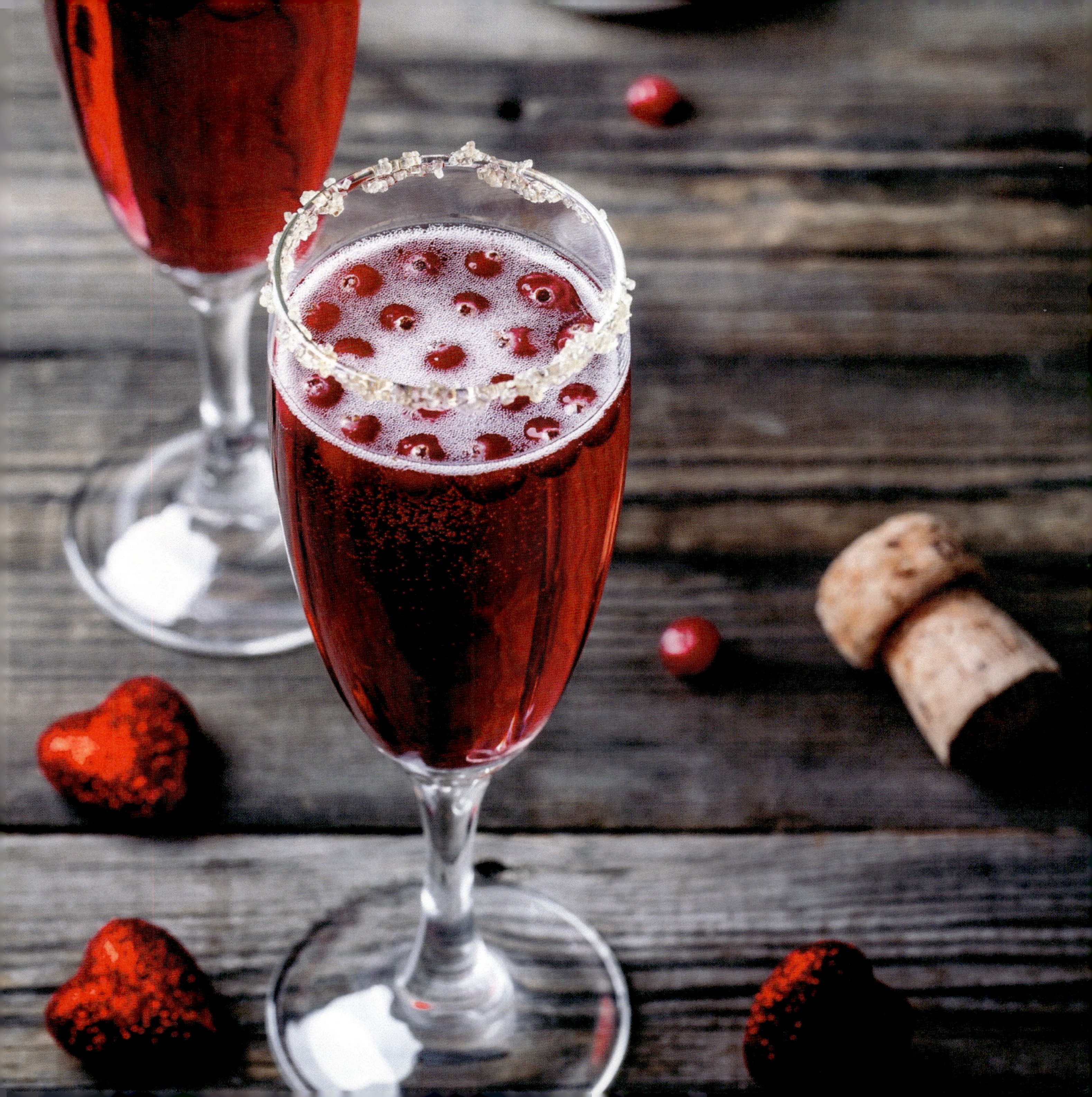

Ingredients Index

A

advocaat 46, 58
almond extract 24
apple 28, 40, 50
apple cider 28
apple juice 40, 50

B

Babycham 46

bourbon whiskey 28, 52
brandy 40, 60
butter 68

C

calvado 18
cardamo 14, 48
cardamom pods 14
champagne 76, 78
chocolate 10, 18, 30, 38, 54, 56, 74
chocolate chip cookie syru 38
chocolate syrup 74
Christmas pudding 62
cinnamon 10, 24, 28, 32, 34, 40, 48, 58
 .... 60, 68, 70
clementine juice 34
clove 48
coffee liqueur 26
cogna 34
Cointreau 14, 64, 66
cranberries, ... 64, 78
cranberry juic 22, 24, 32, 42
cranberry liqueur 78
cream 10, 26, 54, 56, 66, 70, 74
Crème de Cacao, ... 30, 56, 66
Crème de Menth 56

D

dark rum 12, 18, 38, 68

E

egg white 62
egg yol 60
eggnog 74
elderflower cordial 44
espresso 74

G

gin 12, 32, 34, 42, 62
ginger 20, 28, 36, 42, 46, 48, 54
ginger ale 36
ginger beer 20
ginger syrup 46
grapefruit 44
guava juice 16

H

half and half 16, 38
honey 10
hot chocolate 56

I

Irish Whiskey 66

K

Kahlua 38, 54

L

lemon 5, 14, 16, 50, 52, 62, 64
lemon juice 14, 16, 50, 52, 62
lemonade 58
lime 20, 22, 42, 44, 58
lime juice 20, 58, 72

M

maple syrup 18
marmalade 14
milk 10, 18, 60, 66, 70
mincemeat 12
mint leaves 20

N

nutmeg 5, 18, 28, 68, 74

O

orange 5, 14, 22, 24, 30, 34, 40, 44, 48, 52, 62, 76
orange juice 22, 24, 30, 34, 52, 76
orange liqueur 22
orange syrup 30

P

passionfruit 44
peach juice 50
pear cider 32
pear juice 32
Peppermint Schnapps 26, 56
Pimm's 40
pineapple juice 36
pomegranate juic 44
pomegranate syru 22
prosecco 44, 78
pumpkin puree 70

R

red wine 24, 4

S

sloe gin 32
soda water 64
star anise 32
sugar 10, 12, 24, 30, 34, 38, 46, 48, 54, 68, 70, 72
sugar syrup 24, 30, 34, 52, 54, 60, 62

T

triple sec 2

V

vanilla essence 10, 54, 68
vanilla pods 32
vermouth 12, 34
vodka 14, 16, 20, 26, 30, 34, 42, 54

W

water..12, 34, 46, 68
white grape juice 36

X

X Rated Fusion Liqueur 16

Printed in Great Britain
by Amazon